THE MEDIA RELATIONS
Training Handbook

J. Suzanne Horsley
The University of Alabama

Peter M. Macías
Texas State Technical College

WAVELAND
PRESS, INC.
Long Grove, Illinois

For information about this book, contact:
    Waveland Press, Inc.
    4180 IL Route 83, Suite 101
    Long Grove, IL 60047-9580
    (847) 634-0081
    info@waveland.com
    www.waveland.com

To the media relations professionals
who honor the intent of the First Amendment
by setting an example of ethical and transparent
interactions with journalists every day.

J. SUZANNE HORSLEY, Ph.D., is associate professor of public relations and assistant dean of the College of Communication and Information Sciences at The University of Alabama. She is a coauthor of the sixth edition of *On Deadline: Managing Media Relations*. She began her communication career in Virginia working for a decade in state government public affairs and university media relations before joining academia. At Alabama, she teaches courses on public relations, media relations, crisis communication, strategic planning and qualitative research methods. Her communication research in government, crises and disasters has been published in a variety of academic journals and handbooks. The Southern Public Relations Federation named her PR Educator of the Year in 2012.

While a volunteer public affairs spokesperson and trainer with the American Red Cross, Horsley deployed to numerous large-scale disasters where she worked with national and international media that covered the events. In April 2011, she did a "backyard" deployment when an EF4 tornado struck Tuscaloosa, Alabama, destroying 12% of the city. She was recognized for her public information and media relations efforts with several awards, including being named a White House Champion of Change in 2012. She has conducted media training for spokespeople in emergency management agencies and nonprofit organizations around the country.

Horsley is a graduate of the University of Mary Washington (B.A.), Virginia Commonwealth University (M.A.) and the University of North Carolina at Chapel Hill (Ph.D.). She is active in community service and a serial adopter of small dogs.

PETER M. MACÍAS is an accomplished communication executive with more than 30 years of successfully leading and implementing innovative public relations efforts both nationally and internationally. Macías specializes in media relations, crisis communication and reputation management. He is currently the executive director of communication at Texas State Technical College and serves 10 campuses across the state of Texas.

In his last position, Macías served as the communication director for the Service to the Armed Forces division of the American Red Cross. In this position, he was the external affairs liaison to all branches of the U.S. military, the Department of Veterans Affairs and the Department of Defense. During his tenure with the Red Cross, Macías served as a national Red Cross spokesperson during the aftermath of the 9/11 attack on the Pentagon and during numerous large natural disasters. He is a graduate of Southern Illinois University at Edwardsville.

Contents

Preface

We prepared this handbook with both students and working professionals in mind, so you may notice we refer to class project, team, organization or client when discussing the users of this handbook. The book is intended for undergraduate or graduate students studying communication, public relations, strategic communication, marketing or journalism, among other disciplines. It is also designed for communication professionals who are working alone or in teams to develop and implement a media relations training program for their organization.

For readers who are new to media relations, we recommend using *The Media Relations Training Handbook* in combination with *On Deadline: Managing Media Relations*, which covers a broader framework of media relations.[1] Experienced professionals will benefit from our handbook when establishing a new training program for their organization, renovating an existing program or looking to improve aspects of their media training efforts. Our approach to media relations training assumes that you already have a strategic communication plan that guides the work of your organization, team or class project. If not, we recommend you seek more in-depth explanations of media relations and the four-step process of strategic planning.[2]

Whether you are starting from a clean slate or revising an existing media relations training program, our book will take you through a step-by-step guide to develop a robust media training program for your classroom project, business, nonprofit or consultancy—from identifying your key media outlets and writing your talking points to coaching subject matter experts and performing in a mock media interview.

To enhance this step-by-step learning experience, each chapter contains Action Steps designed to build elements of a media training plan. As you complete each Action Step, you advance to the next step in the media relations training process and end up with a comprehensive media relations training guide for your team or organization. Therefore, we recommend that you complete each chapter's Action Steps in order — unless you already have a media training plan in place that simply needs refinement. The digital file of all Action Steps is available for download from the book's page on the Waveland Press website at www.waveland.com.

---

[1] Carole M. Howard, Wilma K. Mathews and J. Suzanne Horsley, *On Deadline: Managing Media Relations*, 6th ed. (Long Grove, Illinois: Waveland Press, 2021).

[2] For more information on incorporating media relations strategies into a strategic communication plan, see Howard, Mathews and Horsley; and Ronald D. Smith, *Strategic Planning for Public Relations* (New York: Routledge, 2017).

Acknowledgments

The authors thank the following contributors for sharing their insights and experiences with the readers of this book:

Jonathan Aiken is the principal at Actuality Media. His expertise in the news industry runs a gamut of journalism positions. He started in radio with anchor/correspondent positions with Associated Press Radio Network and RKO/United Stations/Unistar Radio Networks. Aiken then made the switch to television to be an anchor/correspondent with CNN and CNN International. He then took his experience and used it to support the humanitarian efforts of the American Red Cross as the senior officer of video services.

Renee Felton is a communication professional with 15 years of experience in sports and nonprofit industries. She has worked in collegiate, professional and Olympic athletics. One of the highlights of Felton's career thus far was promoting the U.S. Figure Skating Team leading up to and during the 2014 Olympic Winter Games in Sochi, Russia. She led the communication work for the Dallas Mavericks and is currently with USA Basketball.

Jeanne G. Hamrick, APR, is the director of communications at North American Securities Administrators Association. She is an experienced, successful and award-winning senior strategic communicator with extensive skills in corporate, public, and media relations in the financial, mortgage, humanitarian and education industries. Hamrick, a former journalist, develops and implements communications plans that drive proactive, reactive and interactive communications and outreach strategies to raise awareness, resulting in desired responses and positive actions. Jeanne is a graduate of St. Bonaventure University.

Laura Howe is the senior vice president of global corporate communications for Pearson, a digital learning company with 20,000 employees and education services and products that reach students from K–12 to college and beyond. Her decades-long experience includes being vice president of communications for the American Red Cross National Headquarters, where she led media relations efforts for dozens of national-level disasters and trained a large force of volunteer spokespeople. She started her career in broadcast news and received her journalism degree from the University of Missouri.

Melissa Jackson is an associate professor of mass communications at Piedmont University, located in the North Georgia foothills. She is an Emmy Award-winning storyteller who spent more than 25 years in the broadcast industry producing and supervising newscasts, special broadcasts and documentaries in the Southeast and internationally.

Barry W. Jones, Ph.D., has enjoyed a 40-year career in journalism, public relations and journalism education. He has worked at two newspapers and three universities including Texas A&M University, Mississippi State University and the University of Georgia. He currently lives in Athens, Georgia.

Roger Lowe is the principal at RKL Communication Strategies, LLC. He is a proven and award-winning senior strategic communications leader with the battle-tested blend of experience in high-stakes public affairs campaigns, major crises and proactive brand storytelling along with strong abilities in social, internal and membership engagement for corporate, nonprofit and association clients. Lowe combines his experience as a seasoned print journalist with senior leadership positions in major PR firms such as Porter Novelli and APCO Worldwide and organizations such as the American Red Cross and Grocery Manufacturers.

Scott McBride, commander, U.S. Coast Guard, is the deputy chief of public affairs and former chief of media. He is a type I public information officer and served as a public affairs officer for 13 years. He earned an M.A. in mass communication from UNC Chapel Hill's Hussman School of Journalism and Media, and a B.S. in political science from the United States Naval Academy. He has been a guest lecturer on crisis communication at universities, colleges and government organizations across the country.

Patrick McCrummen's experience and passion drive his life's work to help people move from better days to better lives. Pat joined DuPont in 2018 to build and execute the company's global community impact strategy. Previously, he led global health advocacy and partnership communications at Johnson & Johnson and was VP of communications and marketing for the American National Red Cross. In Delaware, he holds advisory roles with the Wilmington Alliance, United Way of Delaware, the Delaware Racial Justice Collaborative, and Habitat for Humanity of New Castle County. He currently serves as an advisory board member and past chair of the U.S. Chamber of Commerce Foundation Corporate Citizenship Center.

Peggy Wilhide Nasir recently retired from a career of more than 30 years in communication. During that time, she served as press secretary for Vice President Al Gore, deputy CEO for the 2004 Democratic National Convention, associate administrator for public affairs at the National Aeronautics and Space Administration, and vice president for communications at the Association of American Railroads. She spent the last chapter of her career working in international development as a senior external affairs officer at the World Bank Group.

Chris Osborne is the public relations manager for the Jefferson County, Alabama, Department of Public Health. He is a proven communications strategist with more than two decades of broadcast media/PR experience. He specializes in crisis prevention and reputation management. Osborne has managed media relations for multiple large-scale disaster events including Hurricane Sandy, in which he arranged a media opportunity with American Red Cross CEO Gayle McGovern, President Barack Obama, and Secretary of Homeland Security Janet Napolitano. He also enjoys consulting and event planning.

Tammie Pech is an award-winning public relations practitioner with experience in project management, disaster response operations, and large-scale media training. Currently a regional communications and marketing specialist with the USO,

Pech previously served as a regional program manager for the Service to Armed Forces Office of the Red Cross of North Texas. Her specialties include human resources, volunteer management, special event coordination, preparedness and disaster instruction, media relations, social media and photojournalism.

Greg Trevor, associate vice president for marketing and communications at the University of Georgia, has worked in crisis communications for more than two decades. He previously worked at Rutgers, The State University of New Jersey, and The Port Authority of New York and New Jersey. His first-person account of surviving the September 11, 2001, terrorist attacks on the World Trade Center has been republished worldwide.

Dianna Van Horn is an experienced public affairs specialist in nonprofit organization management. She has strong professional skills in nonprofit organizations, photography, crisis communication, editing and volunteer management.

Sadly, **Lawrence Wells** died before this book was published. He was an amazing writer/producer, narrator, teacher, author and innovator. He led small production teams in the field for everything from breaking news to documentary filmmaking. Wells had an extensive background in covering disasters and taught disaster management for both business and public policy. He worked as a senior producer for NBC News and was a five-time Emmy Award nominee. During his more than 30 years of broadcast journalism experience he covered presidential elections, the Challenger Shuttle disaster and wars in Lebanon and Central America. Wells leveraged his knowledge to serve as an adjunct professor at Temple University and as a guest lecturer at Georgetown University.

Katie Wilkes is a Washington, D.C., based writer and storyteller who has been documenting beauty born from crises for more than a decade. She is the author of "The Deep End," a blog inspired by her late rescue dog, which is about life beneath the surface of an empath. Wilkes is a communication consultant for the American Red Cross and has appeared in *The New York Times, The Washington Post,* CNN, *Forbes,* and *USA Today.* She is working on her first memoir.

Expectations of Media Relations Professionals

AGENDA

1. Understand media relations and its role in comprehensive communication programs.
2. Explore the attributes and skills needed by a well-rounded media relations team.
3. Complete the Action Steps at the end of the chapter.

KEY CONCEPTS

Media Relations
Internal Communication
External Communication
PESO Tactics (Paid, Earned, Shared, Owned)
Four-Step Process of Strategic Planning

The Role of Media Relations in a Strategic Communication Program

Media relations is a public relations strategy for communicating about your organization's work through earned media coverage. It is a blend of research, writing, persuasion, public speaking and quick-fire critical thinking. While we often think of our target audiences when planning our efforts in public relations, marketing or advertising, the immediate audience for media relations consists of the journalists, bloggers and other media professionals who produce content for our ultimate target audience.

Media relations work is not done in isolation from other organizational activities. During a crisis event or a major company announcement, for example, the internal and external announcements may need to be simultaneous, depending upon the issue. While media relations can support nearly every communication activity in your organization, it needs to be done in a thoughtful, collaborative and strategic manner.

Figure 1.1 shows how media relations must be incorporated into every aspect of your organization's strategic communication plan. The connection between media relations and **internal communication** is often overlooked, but whether you communicate with employees and volunteers through human resources, corporate communication departments or some other unit, the messaging must be coordinated with all media relations efforts. Employees don't want to learn about the hiring of a new CEO or a lawsuit filed against the company on the news; likewise, employees can be effective brand ambassadors and advocates who amplify strategic messages through word-of-mouth and personal social media accounts.

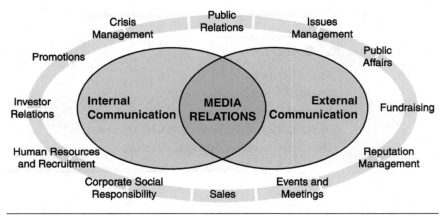

FIGURE 1.1   Integration of media relations with all aspects of the organization's communication strategies.

With **external communication**, the importance of media relations may be a bit more obvious, but it needs careful planning. For example, if you are using a mix of paid advertising and earned media to launch a new product, you should focus on earned media first. Journalists and bloggers will not be interested in announcing your new product if you have already placed ads on television and in trade magazines. In addition, announcements related to publicly traded companies, controlled products (such as pharmaceuticals or alcoholic beverages), quarterly revenue and other financial or investment news may be subject to regulations from federal agencies such as the Securities and Exchange Commission (SEC), the

Federal Trade Commission (FTC) or other regulating agencies. These regulations require collaboration among the media relations team and the investor relations, legal, and government relations teams.

In addition to regulatory concerns, there are many instances in which you need to research legal issues before working with the media. News stories about employees may be subject to privacy laws, and you should always get permission from employees or volunteers before sharing their names or images. Information about criminal activity or civil lawsuits may need to be withheld to protect a law enforcement investigation or litigation process. All these potential issues require that the media relations manager have open lines of communication with all other departments in the organization, including the executive suite.

So, you may be wondering, how does media relations fit within the broader scope of an organization's communication program? **PESO** is a mnemonic device that encapsulates communication plan tactics in four categories: *Paid, Earned, Shared,* and *Owned.* Paid media are advertisements in any form, including the obvious ads on billboards, on television and in print materials; the less obvious purchased editorial materials such as articles in magazines or on blogs; and overtly named sponsorships such as for sporting or charity events. In the paid category, the purchaser has complete control of the content, timing and placement of the messages. On the downside, the audience is smart enough to know that this was paid for and not endorsed by another party.

Earned media are the topics of this book. In the U.S. (as in most democratic countries), journalists are paid by their employers, not by the people they write stories about. If a story makes it onto a cable news program or in a news magazine, for example, it's because the editors and reporters (media gatekeepers) believed the story was worthy of their time and resources to produce it and share with their audiences. Unlike paid media, earned media have the benefit of third-party credibility. However, the organization covered in the story has little to no control over the final product's content, timing or placement.

Shared media are fueled by the larger community. Platforms that support user generated content, such as social media apps, are shared because members of the community can add to, modify or share the content. Finally, owned media are those communication tools that an organization has complete control over, such as websites, newsletters and annual reports.

While each of the PESO categories of tactics (see Figure 1.2) offers advantages and disadvantages for the organization, a comprehensive communication plan is built upon a mix of these approaches. The "Earned Media" column represents media relations tactics. Media relations is just one component of this, but the strategies must be included in a diverse array of message delivery to ensure your intended publics are aware of, understand, remember and act upon your organization's messages. Therefore, while you are researching your public's preferences for media consumption and identifying the best media channels for your pitches, you also want to work strategically with all members of the communication and marketing teams to ensure consistency of messaging across all categories.

	Paid	Earned	Shared	Owned
Examples	Print ads, billboards, TV commercials	News stories, editorials	Social media	Organization websites, videos
Organizational Control	Strong	Weak	Weak	Strong
Advantages for Organization	Determines content, timing and placement; mass distribution	Cost; third-party credibility of media outlet; mass distribution	Cost; quick way to distribute messages; medium allows for variety of visual content	Full control of content, timing, placement and removal or modification
Disadvantages for Organization	Cost; lack of endorsements or implicit credibility	Time consuming; cannot direct content, timing or placement	Public can hijack messages, share out of context, steal copyrighted material, or post contradictory opinions or false information on the organization's sites.	Cost; resource burden for organization; lack of endorsements or implicit credibility

FIGURE 1.2   The PESO model of communication tactics.

Managing the Message With Media Relations

The four types of public relations tactics fit along a continuum depicting how much control the messenger has over the message, as well as how much perceived credibility that message has. On the continuum of message control (see Figure 1.3), organizations have the least control over the message when it is mediated. Media relations, encompassed in the shaded square in Figure 1.3, is a "mediated activity," meaning that another party, an intermediary, is taking your message and then passing it along to the next party. In this case, the media relations spokesperson is the sender of the message, the journalist is the intermediary, and your intended publics eventually receive the message that was produced by the journalist. Journalists will take your information, do additional research, seek alternative perspectives, interpret the information they receive and then produce a story that may or may not support your strategic objectives.

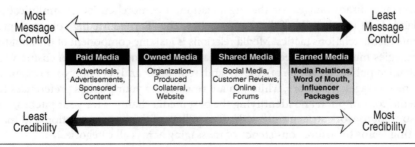

FIGURE 1.3   The PESO model's continuum of control.

However, despite the lack of control, media relations has several benefits. Unlike an advertisement, in which an organization has nearly complete control over the content, timing and location of the message, media coverage provides third-party credibility. Having an objective third-party talking about your organization can appear more credible and trustworthy to the audience. (Note: Some may argue that paid media are less controlled than owned media because you have no influence over the other ads or editorial content that may be in close proximity to your ad; likewise, owned media can be misappropriated and reused for other purposes beyond the organization's control. Therefore, message control may fluctuate in paid and owned media.)

The tactics in each box in Figure 1.3 representing paid, owned, shared and earned media can encompass more than one continuum category; for example, social media are considered "owned" but also "shared" because the public is able to comment on, repost and hijack the messages on these sites. These tactics are rarely implemented in isolation and should be components of strategic plans using a mix of tactics that benefit from multiple approaches to reach the intended audiences.

Qualities of the Media Relations Professional

The relationship between media relations professionals and members of the media is a symbiotic one: each needs the other to be successful. The media relations professional needs the news professional's media outlet to cover and deliver the story to a large audience. The reporter needs the media relations professional as a source for story ideas and accurate information. Relationships with news professionals should be based on mutual respect, timeliness, transparency and accuracy. It is imperative that an updated media roster (next to your communication strategy and Associated Press Style Guide) is within arm's reach when conducting media relations work.

Not all communication professionals are suited for or comfortable with engaging in media relations efforts for their organization. While some people dream of being on camera, others are terrified of doing interviews and prefer to work behind the scenes. The good news is that there is a role in media relations for every personality. Training designed specifically for media relations work is essential for anyone desiring to achieve earned media that supports your organization's objectives. The media training that you will develop through this book will help you discover and sharpen the skills you already have while developing new proficiencies that will benefit you in this competitive communication field.

Successful media relations professionals must be able to demonstrate a multitude of skills simultaneously:

- **Critical Thinking:** Ask questions to determine what needs to be accomplished. Critical thinkers don't take things at face value and are curious to learn more.
- **Strategic and Tactical Communication:** Create a plan and know which communication tools will meet your goals and objectives. This also includes

being aware of the broader news stories (a tactic also known as environmental scanning) that could impact your organization's delivery of products or services. You may also be tasked to outline a problem and provide a solution.

- **Calm Demeanor:** Your actions and attitude will define what type of leader you are and how you will influence your team. News professionals will seek you out as a resource for accurate, timely information.

- **Mindful Forecasting:** In today's 24/7 news cycle, combined with the permanence of the internet, stories are not forgotten. Challenge yourself to see past the initial story, anticipate the reaction and then plan for the second- and third-day stories.

Skills and Personality Traits Inventory

The knowledge, skills and abilities (known as KSAs in human resources lingo) needed for media relations can be aligned with the **four-step process of strategic planning:** research, planning, implementation and evaluation.

A media relations professional may be called upon to serve as spokesperson at a moment's notice, so they must have a solid foundation of knowledge about the organization. In this photo, Peter Macías, former director of communication for Service to Armed Forces at the American Red Cross, addressed the crowd that gathered on the deck of the USS New Jersey in Camden, New Jersey, for the kickoff of the 2019 celebration of "March is Red Cross Month."   **Photo credit: American Red Cross.**

- **Research:** The behind-the-scenes research needed before an interview is ever scheduled can make or break the spokesperson's performance. Research is needed before making proactive pitches as well as before receiving unsolicited media inquiries. A valuable personality trait for researchers is curiosity — what are you interested in learning about this topic? What do you think your target audiences want to know? What do you think the media will be asking about? Successful researchers are proficient in planning and managing investigations; use research from other sources (secondary research); conduct primary research, such as surveys or focus groups; develop analytical skills that allow you to dive into the data while also seeing the big picture; and have excellent reading and writing skills, with the ability to translate complex concepts into clear and concise explanations.

- **Planning:** Interpreting the research and developing a plan to communicate with your selected publics requires high-level strategic thinking and the ability to make connections with other strategic priorities within your organization. Planners make logical ties between what the research has revealed about their issues, products or services, and what will resonate with their publics when developing and communicating organizational messages. This requires strong writing that is persuasive, clear, accurate, ethical and salient for the intended public. The resulting messages articulate the organization's path toward accomplishing its objectives.

- **Implementation:** With research in hand and a plan that supports the organization's objectives, the person charged with implementing the plan must have strong organization and time-management skills, be able to form and lead a team, have strong interpersonal skills to engage with any audience, be able to think critically on their feet under time constraints and be an excellent writer and public speaker. This person must also have in-depth knowledge of the media outlets, journalists and bloggers to whom they will pitch stories and provide interviews. This is where the "relations" comes into "media relations" — developing key relationships with the right media that can add third-party credibility to your organization's news.

- **Evaluation:** Because evaluation is research-based, many of the traits and skills match those of the initial research step. In addition, the evaluator needs to be able to see the big picture, compare the measured results with the intended objectives, be able to write a comprehensive report with justifications for the results and have the interpersonal skills to provide feedback to the individuals who produced the media relations tactics and delivered the media interviews.

ACTION STEPS

As you are learning more about the value of media relations and preparing a training program for your organization, team or class project, it is important to first understand the skills you and your team members bring to the table. Not everyone wants (or needs) to be on a live broadcast interview, and much of the work of media relations happens behind the scenes in research, relationship building, writing, strategic planning, coaching, analytics and evaluation. There is a place for all personality types in media relations, but it is important to do an honest *self-assessment* to help you understand your particular strengths and weaknesses for this type of work. Of course, if you currently hyperventilate when you are about to go on camera, but you really want to improve your interviewing skills, this is the book for you.

Complete the Action Steps to provide the background knowledge you need to move further with development of your media training plan. The Action Steps will help you learn where your strengths lie when it comes to media relations work and start building a well-rounded team that can tackle the various challenges and opportunities in media relations. You may want to revisit this assessment tool later to see how your skillset is developing as you learn more about media relations training.

CHAPTER ONE ACTION STEPS: PERSONALITY AND SKILLS INVENTORY ASSESSMENT

Part A

Complete the chart, rating yourself on a scale of 0-5 (0 means you don't have that trait or skill at all; 3 means you have some familiarity or limited experience with that skill; 5 means you have a strong trait or expertise in that skill). When done, add up the number of points you have for each category. Some attributes are used more than once in this chart.

Personality and Skills Assessment							
A	0-5	B	0-5	C	0-5	D	0-5
Curious		Persuasive		Organized		Analytical	
Attentive to Detail		Strategic		Creative		Attentive to Detail	
Analytical		Working in Teams		Emotional Intelligence[c]		Report Writing	
Reading Comprehension		Writing Skills		Public Speaking		Data Analysis	
Investigative Skills		Time Management		Writing Skills		Able to See the Bigger Picture	
Primary Research[a]		Budgeting		Design and Production		Social Media Analytics	
Secondary Research[b]		Policy Writing		Social Media Management		Evaluative Research	
Data Analysis		Strategic Planning		Website Development		Data Visualization[d]	
Total A:		**Total B:**		**Total C:**		**Total D:**	

[a] Primary research methods include surveys, focus groups, observations, experiments and content analysis. This is original research conducted by you/your organization.

[b] Secondary research includes data that have been previously collected by someone else and are available for free or for purchase, such as journal articles, white papers, news stories, books, survey results and databases.

[c] Emotional intelligence "refers to the ability to identify and manage one's own emotions, as well as the emotions of others."[1]

[d] Data visualization uses spreadsheets or databases to analyze data and then present them in visual forms, such as charts, tables and graphs.

Part B

Add up your scores from Part A to see where your strengths lie in the four steps of strategic planning for media relations discussed on pp. 6-7. If working in teams, include your team members' scores to help determine where your team's overall strengths and weaknesses may be. As you progress through this media training handbook, you will need to ensure you have a well-rounded team in place for achieving the strategic objectives for your project or organization. You may wish to revisit this as you and your team advance though this handbook.

Scores for Personality and Skills Assessment				
Team Member	A Research	B Planning	C Implementation	D Evaluation
Yourself				
Team Member A				
Team Member B				
Team Member C				
Team Member D				
(etc.)				
Total Team Scores:				

REFLECTIONS

1. In which area are you *personally* the most prepared for doing media relations work?
   a. Were you surprised by this result?
   b. Which area do you need or want to develop the most?
2. In which area is your *team*, as a whole, the most prepared for doing media relations work?
   a. Conversely, which areas do you need to develop the most?
   b. Where do your team members' strengths overlap?
   c. What do you think about your team's current level of preparedness for media relations work?

In the Action Steps for the next chapters, we will dive deeper into these concepts and help you and your team learn how to capitalize on the skills you have and develop the ones you need to become a well-rounded media relations team.

NOTE

[1] "Emotional Intelligence," *Psychology Today*, https://www.psychologytoday.com/us/basics/emotional-intelligence, para. 1.

Developing a Media Relations Philosophy and Objectives

AGENDA

1. Develop your organization's media relations philosophy to guide your media training program.
2. Determine the skills needed to conduct media relations.
3. Know how your media relations philosophy may change in a crisis.
4. Complete the Action Steps at the end of the chapter.

KEY CONCEPTS

Media Relations Philosophy (MRP)
Mission, Vision, Values
Crisis

Every Plan Starts With a Philosophy

No matter the size or type of organization you work for, understanding and influencing your organization's **media relations philosophy (MRP)** is vitally important to your communication mission. Similar to the importance of knowing how thrust, lift, drag and weight impact an aircraft's ability to successfully take flight is knowing how a well-developed MRP can help your organization's communication efforts soar.

A written media relations philosophy will guide your media training program; therefore, it should be approved by the executives who oversee external communication functions. This chapter will explore what an MRP should contain, how to construct or revise one for your organization, and why your philosophy needs to be nimble enough to handle crises and changes. Then, we will discuss how to put your philosophy into action.

Who Are You, What Do You Want to Say and Why?

Congratulations! You are embarking on the dynamic portion of your organization's communication strategy. Your goal, as a media relations professional, is to establish and maintain your organization's communication efforts, which accurately tell your company's story through all forms of media. The foundation of a media relations philosophy is built on the answers to three important questions:

- What is the reason for your organization's existence?
- What does your organization plan to accomplish now and in the future?
- What does your organization believe in?

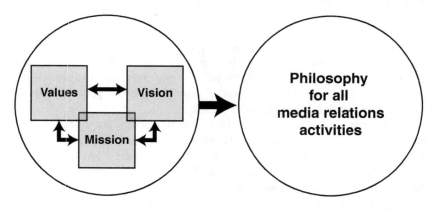

Figure 2.1   The building blocks of a media relations philosophy.

Identifying an organization's **mission** is fairly simple. Is the company for-profit or not-for-profit? What types of manufactured goods does the organization create, or what services does it provide? Does it build trains or do taxes? Does it build skyscrapers or fight for social justice? Does it create delectable confections or deliver retail goods? Does it build computers or help cure cancer?

As your organization's communicator, you become a more credible professional for your colleagues and a valuable resource of information for the public and the news media if you have an acute understanding of your company's mission and its operational intricacies. A starting point for understanding your organization's

MRP is to read the mission statement. The mission statement should communicate to the world what your organization does, how it does it, who the primary stakeholders are, and the impact the organization wishes to make. This statement is short, to the point and coveys how the organization views itself in society. Having a firm understanding of your organizational mission is the first of three foundational steps in wrapping your arms around the company's MRP.

Here are three examples of mission statements from very different organizations:

1. **Google:** To organize the world's information and make it universally accessible and useful.

2. **The Coca-Cola Company:** To refresh the world in mind, body and spirit. To inspire moments of optimism and happiness through our brands and actions.

3. **United States Army:** To deploy, fight, and win our Nation's wars by providing ready, prompt, and sustained land dominance by Army forces across the full spectrum of conflict as part of the Joint Force.

The next step in developing your organization's MRP is understanding your company's **vision** for conducting business now and into the future. How will its products or services impact society? What road map does it have for accomplishing its business goals? Knowing the answers to these questions will help you meet the organization's media relations objectives at the local, state, national or international levels.

One of the greatest challenges for communication professionals is managing episodic versus long-term communication work. Understanding the organization's vision affords you the opportunity to plan and create a media relations strategy and calendar that aligns with the overall corporate mission and vision. You can now establish measurable communication goals that impact your organization's target audience and, in some cases, its bottom line.

It's important to remember that a vision statement looks into the future, and so should your media relations strategy. However, it also needs to be nimble enough to adjust to the inevitable changes that come along. Here are the vision statements of the organizations above. Compare the differences between the mission and vision statements of each organization:

1. **Google:** To provide access to the world's information in one click.

2. **Coca-Cola:** To craft the brands and choice of drinks that people love, to refresh them in body & spirit. And done in ways that create a more sustainable business and better shared future that makes a difference in people's lives, communities and our planet.

3. **United States Army:** To deploy, fight, and win decisively against any adversary, anytime and anywhere, in a joint, multi-domain, high-intensity conflict, while simultaneously deterring others and maintaining its ability to conduct irregular warfare.

The final step in determining your organization's MRP is knowing exactly what it **values.** According to your organization, what are the components that make up the core set of beliefs that serve as a guide for how the media relations team will:

- Work to accomplish the mission?
- Interact internally with each other?
- Interact with the target audience who engages with the organization's products or services?

Many organizations define their values in businesslike ways such as quality, transparency, diversity, integrity, ethics and respect. Other organizations include much broader value concepts such as do no harm, protect the environment, and social justice for all. It is imperative that, at some point, each communicator takes the time to define their professional and personal mission, vision and values and then compares and aligns them with the organization to effectively do their job.

Here are some value statements to review and compare with the matching mission and vision statements:

1. Google's values:
   - Great isn't good enough.
   - Focus on the user, all else will follow.
   - It's best to do one thing really well.
   - Fast is better than slow.
   - Democracy on the web works.
   - You can make money without doing evil.
   - There's always more information.
   - The need for information crosses all borders.
   - You can be serious without a suit.
   - You don't need to be at your desk.
2. Coca Cola's values:
   - Leadership: The courage to shape a better future.
   - Collaboration: Leverage collective genius.
   - Integrity: Be real.
   - Accountability: If it is to be, it's up to me.
   - Passion: Committed in heart and mind.
   - Diversity: As inclusive as our brands.
   - Quality: What we do, we do well.
3. United States Army's values:
   - Loyalty: Bear true faith to the Constitution, the Army, your unit and other soldiers.
   - Duty: Fulfill your obligations.
   - Respect: Treat people the way they should be treated.
   - Selfless Service: Put the welfare of the nation, the Army and your subordinates before your own.
   - Honor: Live up to Army Values.
   - Integrity: Do what is right, legally and morally.
   - Personal Courage: Face fear, danger or adversity (physical or moral).

Connecting Media Relations to Organizational Strategy

Media relations is part of an organization's overall communication strategy. A communication professional must be able to create and execute a plan that forecasts strategic media outreach for the year, and the plan must be flexible enough to change based on unforeseen internal and external factors that could impact the organization. In Chapter 4 we will take you through the research process to develop goals and objectives that will guide your media relations strategies.

Media relations affords communication professionals the opportunity to employ their strategic professional abilities on behalf of their organization, use storytelling skills to share the organization's messages, develop relationships with members of the news media and influence stakeholders to act based upon the information they shared with the public. As an example, many people who see disaster stories on the news featuring the American Red Cross perceive it to be an organization that only operates in crises such as hurricanes, earthquakes and tornadoes. In reality, the scope of the Red Cross mission includes not only disaster response, but collecting almost half of the nation's blood supply, providing service to the armed forces, delivering health and safety training and much more. Issues such as a severe drop in financial donations, a crisis of ethics or a perceived breakdown in quality service delivery could derail the organization's everyday media relations efforts. Therefore, media relations specialists must tell the complete story of the Red Cross to ensure better public understanding of the full mission.

Storytelling

Your work to understand your organization's mission, vision and values will be the foundation of all your stories. Storytelling, the ability to engage the public with your organization's message in a meaningful way, is an art form, and it consists of three parts:

1. Create a compelling story based on timely and relevant issues/events/ people in the community, state or country that highlights your organization's mission.
2. Entice the news media to want to tell this story.
3. Ensure that the story resonates with the target public in a way that motivates them to act.

Beyond the who, what, why, when, where and how, the real question to ask is what are you trying to accomplish with your story — are you selling more product, launching a new service, collecting donations or just trying to generate awareness that in some way will serve the community? What story are you sharing with the public that moves them to act based upon the information you've shared with them? How are you connecting this story to your mission, vision and values?

Peggy Nasir is an experienced media relations professional who has led communication programs from the White House to the World Bank. But even she needed to go back to her training to survive a crucial mistake during a seemingly innocuous interview. Your efforts must be continuous to prepare for interviews and make connections between your media relations philosophy and your storytelling. Nasir shares her story of why you can never be prepared enough, even for a standard media interview.

Why Preparation Is Important for Every Interview, No Matter How Early in the Morning

I never was a morning person. Getting up to do early morning television interviews was always my least favorite part of my job.

Maybe that was the reason I didn't prepare for what was supposed to be a relatively easy interview with a Washington, D.C., television station during the second inauguration of President Bill Clinton in January 1997. Scheduled for the early morning hours between 6 and 7 a.m., the interview was about the festivities leading up to the president's swearing-in ceremony.

Easy, I thought. I could talk about the parade, the fireworks, the thousands of people coming from all over the country to witness the event. I knew most of the information off the top of my head: the length of the parade route, the number of marching bands and the lineup of entertainment.

One of the highlights of this particular inauguration — at least in the minds of those who put these kinds of events together — was a fireworks display that could be seen from anywhere in the city. Always mindful of a "news hook," we made a big deal of the fact that, for the first time, the inauguration would feature a fireworks display that could be seen from every vantage point in the city. I forwarded to the television station a couple of fact sheets, including a television-friendly map of the best locations to watch the fireworks.

Then I made a critical error. I didn't prepare for the interview. I thought it would be a walk in the park. And it would have been had I bothered to prepare before I went on.

It started off well enough. Plenty of easy questions about the upcoming event. Then came a question that should have been easy:

"Where are the best places to watch the fireworks," asked the morning news anchor.

"All over the city," I replied.

"But can you give us some specific locations?"pressed the anchor.

"Ummm, from anywhere," I replied.

"Anywhere?" asked the dubious anchor."But can you tell us where the best viewing spots will be?"

"Ummm, Capitol Hill, Catholic University," I mumbled, scrambling to recall any elevated ground in the metro D.C. area."Really anywhere. I sent you a map."

The minute I said those words, I sent you a map, I knew I had bombed. Not on a hard question, but over fireworks. It's a lesson I've never forgotten. Always prepare. Never wing it. No matter how early in the morning. No matter how easy it looks.

Crisis Matters — A Lot!

A **crisis** is any issue or event that catches you off guard and derails the organization's normal daily routine — a hurricane, a tornado, a lapse in ethics, a significant decline in product quality or service delivery, or even a pandemic. Of the many incidents that test an organization's mettle, a crisis and how successfully the organization responds to that crisis can make or break the organization's reputation and bottom line. This is why understanding an organization's MRP and having a good plan helps mitigate the impact of a crisis.

The initial step in creating the crisis communication plan, which should be quick and easy, is to understand the mission, vision and values (especially the values) of the organization. The same mission, vision and values that you determined for your overall MRP are still in play.

How and when the organization communicates with stakeholders during a crisis will predict the organization's reputational outcome. The hallmark concepts for a good MRP include: honesty, transparency, demonstration of remorse, timely actions and a willingness to do what is right for all stakeholders. The ability to deliver timely and accurate information to the public during a crisis establishes a communicator's credibility and the organization's dedication to doing what is best for the stakeholders.

The second part of a crisis communication plan includes research. A communicator can prepare for a crisis by conducting an internal self-assessment — identifying areas of the organization susceptible to exposure that may result in a crisis, such as cultural vulnerabilities, fiscal vulnerabilities, industrial vulnerabilities or human resource vulnerabilities.

The third part of the crisis communication plan ensures that all the tools necessary to get the job done are at your fingertips. Here are a few items you may consider for your toolkit:

- An up-to-date media roster.
- The latest telephone roster for the leadership team.
- Key messages and updated talking points.
- Frequently asked questions.

Crisis communication is a team activity. The fourth part of the plan is to assemble a group of people to be part of the crisis communication team. The team does not have to be a large number of people, but its members must represent different parts of the organization and be able to think through the situation and provide feedback to resolve the issue/event. The team should include, but is not limited to:

- Representatives of the leadership team: chief executive officer, chief operating officer, human resources lead or chief financial officer.
- Subject matter experts from across the organization (especially ones you can rely on for technical information and for interpreting that information for a general audience).
- The communication team.
- The designated spokesperson.

Although a professional communicator cannot prepare for every possible crisis, conducting periodic spokesperson training and simulated crisis exercises can help prepare the team for potential crises. Systematic media training ensures that someone is always prepared and ready to respond when the time comes.

ACTION STEPS

As you learn more about the mission, vision and values of your organization, you can begin to add this information to your media relations training program. This important background information will guide the development of your training objectives and materials.

Complete the Action Steps for this chapter, which asks you to do some personal reflection as you consider how your personal philosophy aligns with that of your employer. Develop your personal mission, vision and values, and then compare them to those of the client or organization you are working for.

CHAPTER TWO ACTION STEPS: MISSION, VISION AND VALUES

Part A

Create your own *personal* mission, vision and values statements. Follow the guidelines and examples from the chapter.

My Mission: _____

My Vision: _____

My Values: _____

Part B

Fill in the statements for your *organization*. Hopefully, your organization already has these in place, but if not, this is a good opportunity to start drafting them.

Organization Mission: _____

Organization Vision: _____

Organization Values: _____

Part C

Reflect on how your personal statements compare to those of your organization as you respond to these questions:

1. Where do you and your organization agree, and where are there differences?_____

2. Do the value statements of your organization resonate with you personally, and why or why not? _____

3. Are there any values held by your organization that are in conflict with your personal values? If so, how will you navigate those differences as you serve in a publicly facing media relations role for your organization?_____

4. As you develop your media relations training program, what are some ways that you can incorporate the mission, vision and values in your training materials and interview simulations?_____

5. Share your answers with your team members and discuss what changes you would recommend, if any, for your organization's statements. _____

Selling the Media Relations Philosophy to Leadership

AGENDA

1. Understand why it is critical for communicators to have a seat at the leadership table.
2. Recognize how the media relations plan will support the mission, vision and values of your organization.
3. Learn how to secure consensus and approval from executive leadership for the media relations philosophy, plan and training.
4. Identify ways a media relations plan can support ethical decision-making.
5. Complete the Action Steps at the end of the chapter.

KEY CONCEPTS

Ethics

Trust, Accuracy, Competence and Timeliness (T.A.C.T.)

Reputation Management

Key Stakeholder Audit

Getting Buy-in From the Leadership Team

You've just completed some very serious research into the mission, vision and values for both yourself and your organization. You are resolved in the fact that the media relations philosophy you've created or updated is a solid foundation from which to conduct the organization's media relations mission for routine as well as nonroutine matters.

It's time to start planning your training sessions — but not so fast. There are three tasks that need immediate attention: First, learn how your organization is perceived in the media and in the community. This will help determine if your media relations philosophy and newly minted media plan successfully support your organization's mission, vision and values. It will also help you focus your training on key issues that you have identified.

The communication mission, and especially the media relations mission, is a team sport, even if the communicator is a shop of one. Therefore, the second task is to ensure that consensus and approval have been secured from the organization's leadership and operational/service leaders regarding the MRP, plan and training program. To put this in journalistic terms, the team needs to understand and be comfortable with the who, what, where, when, why and how — especially the why — of the MRP and the resulting plan. Helping the team understand the "why" gets to the heart of the media plan: its proposed results, timelines, resources, contingencies and benefits. It's important because your executives and all team members will be approving your resources (as you will see in Chapter 6) and may be playing the role of spokesperson.

And third, you must understand that **ethics** plays a key role in media relations. You are a relationship manager and must engage your key stakeholders, both internal and external, from a platform of trust, accuracy, competence and timeliness. These attributes are important in a communicator's everyday work life and

---

| **Insights From a Media Relations Pro** | *A missed deadline with the press is a missed opportunity to connect your organization with current issues and make it relevant in the community. Barry Jones, a retired media relations professional and former journalism educator, shares his experience with trust in media relations work.* |

The Process of Building Relationships With Media

Every organization has publics (clients, customers, audiences) that are important to them and to which they are accountable. One of the many important ways these publics can be reached is through media. But media arrive at this equation with a built-in skepticism and (usually) an adversarial attitude. This is and probably always will be a tenuous relationship. However, it is not an impossible one.

The relationship is made more probable through the simple process public relations practitioners call *media relations*. This process is based on being a reliable, truthful and trustworthy partner with media in the flow of information. When media relations ethical issues arise, it is most often over questions about reliability, truthfulness or trust that has broken down between public relations practitioners and media professionals.

This makes reliability, truthfulness and trust the essential foundation for any media relations strategist seeking to establish a reputation as a partner. Such a partnership is rendered best by being a source dedicated to truth and being a trusted source of information. Acquiring a valued reputation demands years of time and energy. Along the way, the practitioner becomes a connection between the organization and the media leading to credible experts, opinions or data needed to write powerful stories.

even more important when the organization is faced with a crisis or is presented with an ethical dilemma.

Organizational ethics are apparent in the mission, vision and values statements of your organization, and ethics will be an integral part of the media relations training you provide for your team, executives and subject matter experts. Whether you are conscious of it or not, your ethics will influence how you treat your colleagues, how you work with the media, who you trust and how transparent you are when answering questions.

Words and Actions Can Make or Break a Professional Communicator

When the public is exposed to a never-ending barrage of scandals on the 24/7 news and in ubiquitous social media, the public relations profession is sometimes viewed as *those people* who are trying help their clients or organization weasel out of issues and crises through a lack of transparency, half-truths, blame deflection, unsubstantiated innuendoes and outright lies. At the heart of a communicator's work is the relationships they build and continually maintain with their key stakeholders. As Roger Lowe, an experienced communication executive, often says, "your words and your actions matter." The

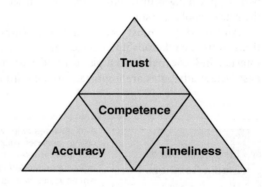

FIGURE 3.1   THE T.A.C.T. MODEL OF TRUST, ACCURACY, COMPETENCE AND TIMELINESS.

reputation of a quality professional communicator is based on T.A.C.T.: Trust, Accuracy, Competence and Timeliness (see Figure 3.1).

Every professional communicator wants to help their organization grow and be successful. The organization's key stakeholders are relying on the person leading the communications effort to conduct themselves in an ethical business-like manner by building a foundation of **trust**: trust that the communicator is conducting quality work, trust that the organization's mission, vision and values are at the forefront of a communicator's mind, and trust that the media are turning to the communicator as a subject matter expert and valuable source.

Everyone makes a mistake now and then; but when communicating on behalf of your organization or client, exactness of information, transparency and honesty will help you as a communication professional be known and relied upon for your **accuracy**. News professionals will turn to you knowing that the information and stories you are sharing need very little to no verification. Plus, with the reputation of being a provider of accurate information, the media relations professional will be a sought-after subject matter expert on topics related to your organization, issue or industry.

A successful communication professional displays the ability to do quality work, be creative and be efficient. They display a level of **competence** that distinguishes them through the use of critical thinking skills, adaptability of their efforts when situations change, creative approaches to accomplishing their mission, and dedication to the highest standards of the public relations profession.

The public's consumption of news and information seems to be insatiable. The news outlets are in an all-out sprint to satisfy the public's need for news and information and provide it as quickly as possible. A reporter's race with the clock to meet deadlines is now shorter than ever. For professional communicators, **timeliness** is an important part of the relationship between reporters and media relations professionals. It's just as important as the quality and accuracy of the information being shared with the reporter.

Insights From a Media Relations Pro	*Patrick McCrummen is an experienced communicator who has shaped media relations programs for national nonprofits, global corporations and advisory boards. He shares his experience of earning the support and trust of organizational leaders for his media relations training efforts.*

Engaging Leadership in Your Communication Strategy for Reputation Management

Reputation management and *communication strategy* are inextricably linked in our discussions of media relations. Reputation is continually assessed based on the perception of how your organization addresses people's expectations over time. A solid communication strategy considers an environment in which perceptions can change instantly — either positively or negatively — and how you continually address these expectations. Whether by one person, an organized group or a groundswell of public opinion, identifying those who have the highest potential to influence your organization is critical.

But consider, too, the extent to which reputation is shaped by the actions of influencers INSIDE your organization — typically those in power and who have enough influence over the organization to guide its ethos, purpose, philosophy, decisions and actions.

No matter the size of your organization, it is important to understand the perspectives of these key internal stakeholders, such as board members, senior leadership and key function leaders.

If you're new to the organization, it's fairly easy to make a case for these interviews as part of the strategy development and onboarding process. If you've been there a while, consider this work as part of a **key stakeholder audit,** which gives you permission to ask a series of structured questions that may seem awkward during informal conversations.

Why is this so important? There are several reasons. First, along with your deep research and the key stakeholder audit, this work forms the foundation of your reputation management strategy, which must, in turn, inform your media training philosophy.

(continued)

Second, engaging key internal leaders allows you as the communication leader to gauge what each member appreciates about the role of communication, its influence on reputation and the value of communication generally, and how they perceive your role's ability to create their perceived level of value. In other words, will they afford you a seat at the table?

Another important reason is that you, as the communication leader, are creating (if you're new to the organization) or dimensionalizing your credibility through these conversations, even if informal, and assessing the environment under which all your work will be influenced. Approach these conversations with openness and humility, while listening intently for key points of view. You'll be amazed by how much you learn (and whether or not your first impressions of this person were on the mark!).

Finally, building a simple map of key perspectives across your key stakeholder interviews is a valuable exercise. It synthesizes the top few insights about each person into a picture of your influencer ecosystem. You can also overlay this work with your external stakeholders — which serves to help you understand who your key influencers are and how their influence is channeled in your community.

Along with your deep research and the key stakeholder audit, you will have a solid foundation for your communication strategy and everything you need to craft your media relations training plan with the support of your leadership team. Your efforts will help crystallize your communication goals, prioritize key stakeholders and lay the groundwork for a sustainable and credible strategy to generate positive sentiment.

Securing a Seat at the Decision-Making Table

Despite what some business professionals believe, it is vitally important for an organization to ensure that a professional communicator is a member of the leadership team and has a seat at the organization's decision-making table. It has been established repeatedly that a key trait of a quality leader is effective communication.[1] We would venture to say that effective communication is also a key trait of a quality leadership team. It's for that reason that an organization's communication professional should be an integral part of the leadership team. The communicator is there to serve as communication counsel first by listening to and then by synthesizing information and sharing ideas on how the communication process should be conducted in support of the organization's mission, vision and values. The communicator must be able to forecast possible media and reputational issues that can both positively and negatively impact their organization, while serving as the conduit of information to all key stakeholders.

ACTION STEPS

Now that you have identified your organization's media relations philosophy in Chapter 2, the next challenge is to gain the support of your leadership team.

Complete the Action Steps for this chapter, which guide you through development of your strategy to gain support from leadership for your media relations philosophy.

CHAPTER THREE ACTION STEPS:
SECURING CONSENSUS AMONG YOUR LEADERSHIP TEAM
FOR THE ORGANIZATION'S MEDIA RELATIONS PHILOSOPHY

Part A

You've investigated and determined your organization's media relations philosophy, and it's a philosophy that you can embrace and can execute. Now it's time to build consensus with your organization's leadership. This support and agreement from executives will be necessary as you build your team with spokespeople and subject matter experts, but also when it's time to seek approval for resources to conduct your training. Let's start by assessing the opportunities and threats from the leadership in your or your client's organization.

1. The simplest way to exchange information with your organization's leadership is by interviewing and meeting with them. What would this meeting look like? Would you conduct a team briefing to get group buy-in and then meet with each of them individually? Do you have the time to do this? _____

2. List at least four examples of the leadership traits you identified within your organization that could positively or negatively impact your MRP, and then describe how you would you address them. Here are some samples of organizational traits that you may encounter:

   a. The press is the enemy and not to be trusted.

   b. Our organization's information is proprietary and cannot be shared.

   c. Executives with approval authority don't understand the need for a timely exchange with the news media.

   d. Leaders don't understand the need for open and accurate communication with external and internal audiences.

   e. Executing the MRP will prevent all crises for our organization.

3. There will be members of your leadership team who will immediately understand what you're trying to accomplish with the MRP. How would you go about engaging *their* support to amplify your message and build consensus among all executives for the MRP? _____

4. What does your seat at the leadership table look like? What are your expectations when engaging with the members of the leadership team? _____

Part B

Now that you have identified opportunities and threats from your organization's leadership, draft a plan for how you will approach the leaders to gain their support for your media relations training plan.

NOTE

[1] Anchal Luthra and Richa Dahiya, "Effective Leadership Is All About Communicating Effectively: Connecting Leadership and Communication." *International Journal of Management and Business Studies* 5, no. 3 (September 2015). https://www.mcgill.ca/engage/files/engage/effective_leadership_is_all_about_communicating_effectively_luthra_dahiya_2015.pdf

Using Research and Planning to Build Your Media Relations Strategy

AGENDA

1. Understand how the public views legacy media.
2. Identify media that your target publics follow.
3. Evaluate the media coverage you already have.
4. Identify goals and objectives for creating a media relations strategy.
5. Learn how to conduct a communications audit and how this research will help your media training participants.
6. Complete the Action Steps at the end of the chapter.

KEY CONCEPTS

Legacy Media
Third Party Credibility
Media Lists
External Communication Audit
S.M.A.R.T. Objectives
Media Audit

Not Your Mother's Media Environment

Media relations has always been an important part of any organization's communication plan, but the nature and environment of media relations work have changed significantly over time. Just in recent years, the public's trust in **legacy media** (also known as traditional media, such as broadcast and print news, whether in their original form or posted online) has declined. The 2020 Edelman Trust Barometer found that only 47% of the general population trusted the media.[1] This widespread distrust of media, combined with social media's perpetuation of fake news and deepfakes (videos altered to make it appear that a public official said things they did not say), has made the public seek their news and information from sources they agree with, not necessarily from sources that are objective and unbiased.[2]

Because of these issues with trust, communication plans include media relations strategies to balance the effect of third-party credibility. **Third-party credibility** simply means that an unrelated entity has "endorsed" your organization, products, services or issues by spending the time and resources to conduct their own research and reporting. This type of endorsement is not the same as an advertisement telling you to buy or do something; in this case, it means the media organization has found your news story to be worthy of being reported and shared with their readers, viewers or listeners. The media outlet then spends its time, money and resources to produce and distribute the story.

This also does not mean that the reporter agrees with you, supports your organization's work or even gets the story completely right. All it means is that a reporter did their own research, possibility sparked by your pitch or news release, to write a story in which they also must balance it with other viewpoints or perspectives. The responsibility is on the media relations professional who is providing information and preparing spokespeople or subject matter experts to go on the record with the reporter.

Add the effort required to attract a journalist's attention with the public's negative perception of media, and you have a significant challenge for even the most seasoned media relations professional. They must adjust their strategies for earning media coverage while also ensuring that they have a comprehensive communication plan for reaching their intended audiences. These challenges, while daunting, are not insurmountable, and this handbook will guide you through a process to help your team be prepared for today's media climate.

Media training is important now, more than ever, to ensure that your organization benefits from fair and accurate media reporting and is prepared when adversity strikes. With these caveats, let's explore how to address the current challenges of the news media industry in your media relations training program.

"To Whom It May Concern" Concerns No One

Veteran reporters will gleefully share stories of the mountains of news releases they received from vacuous public relations pros over the past decades. Staid announcements of various degrees of value would randomly appear in the mail, by fax, over newswires, and, today, in email junk folders. Even when a news release was truly newsworthy, it was still difficult for the reporters to cut through the mass-distributed releases and identify good story opportunities for their audiences.

Once email became the most common means of distributing news releases and pitches, media relations pros were coached on how to write eye-catching, jaw-dropping subject lines that would resonate with the reporter and convince them to open the email and, at a minimum, read it. This led to more cynicism by journalists who were tired of the sales pitches. The competition generated by a large pool of media relations professionals for the attention of a steadily shrinking pool of journalists makes it challenging to get your pitches to turn into stories.

The days of mass distributed "To Whom it May Concern" generic emails are long gone, thanks to the sheer amount of information that is constantly circulating to newsrooms and editorial desks. The process of developing, updating and/or maintaining your proactive media lists (depending upon how mature your media lists already are) will also help those in your media relations training program better understand the importance of these relationships and of relating to the goals of the reporters you seek out. Effective media relations strategies start with selecting media channels that:

1. your intended audience follows;
2. will be interested in covering your story or issue; and
3. have reported on your subject matter fairly, accurately and ethically.

These criteria may seem unrealistic given that media relations experts also must deal with media outlets that may not pass this test. However, when you are developing a media list of key reporters with whom you will proactively work to develop relationships, you want it to be as targeted to your strategic objectives as possible.

Alternatively, every organization has a secret (or not so secret) "Do Not Call" list of media outlets that have given them issues in the past. Perhaps these reporters never take your calls, have made factual errors in previous stories or have presented an unfair or biased account of your issues. It's equally important for those in the media training program to understand how to identify and work with antagonistic media. This is where we add the fourth criteria to our list for media channel selection:

4. Your intended audience follows this media outlet, even if it's *not favorable* to your strategic objectives.

Media channel selection should be part of your ongoing media relations training as you work to enhance your **media lists** and conduct meaningful training exercises that hit the target, which is your key media stakeholders. Your media relations training program can help your spokespeople and SMEs understand why generic pitches and "throwing Jell-O at the wall" are not good strategies for gaining media coverage that will benefit your organization.

Likewise, relying on the same friendly reporter who always takes your pitches may not have an impact on your intended target audience. Most importantly, considering how divided the U.S. public is over media preferences these days, media channel selection is a critical conversation to have with your MR teams.

A Note on Friends and Anti-Friends

Like Mom always said, "The friends you hang out with are a reflection of you." Media relations professionals want their organizations to earn positive, fair, accurate and complete coverage of their issues. Association with a media outlet that doesn't share your organizational values or has an agenda against you or your industry may not have a positive outcome for your stakeholders.

While our #4 reason above for adding an outlet to your media lists may seem to contradict our other reasons, the adage "keep your friends close and your enemies closer" should be posted in every media relations manager's office as a reminder: A biased selection of media on your part will *always* eliminate the opportunity for your voice to be heard in an opposing story. *When you don't speak, someone else will always fill the void.* Your goal should be to represent your organization or issue to the best of your ability and never forego an opportunity to present your side of a story.

To help everyone on your media relations team (which includes your organizational leadership and subject matter experts) understand how your organization is currently viewed and treated by the media, it's time to assess your media coverage results and refine your training strategies moving forward.

Where Are We Going and How Are We Getting There?

The only way to determine whether all the hard work you've put into creating your media relations plan is effective is by conducting more research — in this case, an external communication audit. An **external communication audit** is a useful tool for determining your organization's public reputation and the viability of your organization's communication mission (in this case, the media relations plan). It's a quick look, at a particular point in time, at how your target audiences are perceiving your organization. It lets the communicator know if the messaging, print collateral, graphics and communication delivery vehicles are working, or if they need to be retooled.

There are usually two ways to approach an external communication audit. The first is to hire an outside organization that specializes in this type of work. The cost of hiring an outside firm to conduct an external communication audit may range from thousands to tens of thousands of dollars depending on the size of the organization and the complexity of the scope of the work. For a smaller organization that operates on a limited budget, and certainly for a classroom experience, hiring an outside firm is cost prohibitive. So, the second option for conducting an external communication audit is to conduct a self-assessment. This option will involve some time and extra effort but will take the smallest hit on your departmental budget.

A quality communication audit will help communicators determine:

- How the communication mission was articulated in the past.

- Who your organization's target audiences are and how they are receiving your messages.
  - ☐ What is the current perception of the products and services offered by your organization?
  - ☐ What information does the communicator need to share with the target audiences and how would these audiences prefer to consume that information?
- What is currently working or not working in your media plan.
- Where the unrecognized opportunities may be for future media relations efforts.

Ultimately, the external communication audit will help identify where the organization's communication efforts are most robust and where there is need for improvement.

Here are a few steps to help you start conducting a communication audit (external and internal):

1. **Identify the scope of the audit:** For the media relations plan, the communicator needs to determine who the target audiences are:
   a. External media relations stakeholders — print journalists, broadcast journalists, bloggers, trade publications, online influencers
   b. Internal stakeholders — the organization's leadership, department leads, subject matter experts, and employees or volunteers

2. **Gather samples for review:**
   a. Old news releases
   b. Messages
   c. Feature stories
   d. Media calendar

3. **Ask questions and collect feedback by using primary research:[3]**
   a. Electronic surveys
   b. Focus groups
   c. Individual interviews

4. **Determine strengths, weakness, opportunities and threats (SWOT; see Figure 4.1):**
   a. Strength — what communication tactics are working well?
   b. Weakness — what communication tactics haven't work and need to be retooled?
   c. Opportunities — what opportunities have been identified to help improve communication efforts?
   d. Threats — what factors threaten the organization's effort to effectively communicate with stakeholders?

5. **Analysis and recommendations:**

   a. Prepare an analysis document that describes an overall look at the organization's communication effort — good and bad.

   b. Provide a set of suggestions to improve the organization's communication efforts.

   c. Include a plan to make and implement changes with attainable objectives and a reasonable time frame for completion.

After you collect and analyze the data from your communication audit, identify the strengths, weaknesses, opportunities and threats for your organization that may affect the viability of your media relations plan.

Strengths What advantages do you have?	**Weaknesses**· What disadvantages do you have?
Opportunities What could you do to build upon the strengths you have or improve your weaknesses?	**Threats** What could harm or interfere with your organizational goals?

FIGURE 4.1   SWOT matrix.

Media Relations Goals and Objectives

Clear and measurable outcomes are the building blocks for a successful media relations strategy. Although the terms "goals" and "objectives" are sometimes used interchangeably, there is a significant difference between them: A goal is a broad statement identifying business outcomes over a period of time — one to three years. Objectives are specific, singular steps you will take to work toward your overarching goal.

A useful tool for creating a solid media relations strategy is **S.M.A.R.T. objectives.** S.M.A.R.T.[4] is an acronym that stands for **specific, measurable, attainable, relevant** and **time-bound.** S.M.A.R.T. was originally used to help business professionals set goals and objectives for project management work. This tool is easily adaptable for media relations as it's easy to understand and measure your success.

Here's an example of a media relations *goal* for a nonprofit healthcare agency:

- Become a credible and reliable information resource about diabetes for the local community.

To reach this goal, consider these possible *objectives:*

- Offer at least three community diabetes education sessions per year that are taught by your staff.

- Earn coverage of these education sessions in at least 75% of local news media outlets by the close of the 12-month period.

Both of these objectives support the larger goal of establishing the agency as an important information resource in the community. In addition, each objective focuses on a specific action, has a defined timeframe and has a measurement goal. Your prior research and experience will tell you if these objectives are attainable and relevant. Based upon your agency's workload, are three community education events per year possible? And based upon your prior media coverage, would you be able to reasonably receive coverage in 75% of your local media outlets? If you can answer the S.M.A.R.T. questions for your objectives, you can then justify your strategic plan to your supervisors and leadership team.

Specific	Clearly identify a singular objective that you wish to accomplish.
Measurable	Define your objective so that you have a meaningful way to measure your results.
Attainable	The objective should be realistic, manageable and affordable.
Relevant	The objective is important to achieving your overall organizational goals.
Time-bound	You have a clearly defined time frame from implementation to measurement.

FIGURE 4.2   How to write S.M.A.R.T objectives.

Drilling Down Into Your Data To Bolster Your Media Lists

Once you have conducted your external communication audit, it's time to focus on the media results to see how they align with your existing plan. A **media audit** is a subset of the external communication audit. This deep examination of your media coverage will help you analyze your media relations efforts in a systematic way by:

- Providing a *count* of news stories about your organization or your issue/industry in a specified timeframe.
- Estimating the *reach* (i.e., number of views, geographic scope, or audience demographics) of these news stories.
- Revealing the *news outlets and reporters* who cover your organization or issues the most often.
- Highlighting *other organizations* competing with you for news coverage.
- Discovering the *sentiment* (positive, negative or neutral) of these news stories toward your organization or issue.
- Identifying the *friends and anti-friends* that you need to be most aware of.

It is also important to understand the type and sentiment of news coverage that your organization is already receiving. If your organization never appears in a Google news search, then you are starting from the basics. If your organization already has adequate news coverage or has experienced a recent crisis, you may need to refine your strategies, train new spokespeople or adjust the way you target your media outlets.

Much like the larger external communication audit, organizations can conduct this media audit on their own by using free online search engines, by hiring a firm that specializes in media audits or by subscribing to commercially available media databases.[5] The Action Steps at the end of the chapter will get you started; for more detailed information on and examples of measuring and evaluating media relations efforts, see Chapter 10 of *On Deadline: Managing Media Relations.*[6]

Once you have a snapshot of your media coverage results, return to your media relations plan to see if you are achieving your goals. Which areas need the most work? Are reporters showing an understanding of your organization's mission? Are other voices dominating the coverage and preventing your organization from telling its story? Can you identify which spokespeople from your organization did the best job of delivering key messages? What are the primary rumors or bits of misinformation that you will need to address in future interviews? What have you done well? Remember to celebrate the victories as much as you fret over the losses.

With the media audit in hand, take a fresh look at your media lists. Do your media lists match up with the resulting coverage? Which reporters or news outlets have you missed entirely? Who is covering your organization and/or your issue the most — your friends or your anti-friends? Are your media lists hitting the bullseye, touching on any portion of your target, or have you completely missed your target?

Incorporating Your Analyses Into Your Training

Now it's time to add what you've learned from your external communication audit and your media audit to your media relations training program.

Share the Results. Media relations training should be conducted with a realistic foundation. Bring all training participants up to speed on stakeholder perceptions, your SWOT results, and the current state of your news coverage — the good, the bad and the ugly. Share your media audit findings with the team. Help them understand what has worked, what hasn't and how all this supports your media relations philosophy. Provide story examples to read or view, offer profiles of reporters who have helped or hindered your strategic objectives and hold open discussions of how to tackle issues in future interviews.

Reenact the Coverage. Invite training participants to revisit some of the past news coverage by re-creating the interviews. Use these "Monday morning quarterbacking" opportunities to practice and reinforce interview strategies that can help interviewees tell the story in a more effective way in the future. You can also use old media coverage to design the scenarios you will build in Chapter 11 so that your simulations will be grounded in facts familiar to all training participants.

Solicit Their Expertise. Remember that every member of your media relations team is there because of their expertise. Ask the training participants for their insights on why news stories may have turned out the way they did. What would they do differently next time? Ask them if the media *they* read and watch for industry news were included in your media audit. Have you missed out on opportunities to tell your story via an overlooked media channel that may be preferred by your target publics? Have you neglected a media strategy that would resonate with those who want to learn more about your industry or issue? Experts within your own organization will have great insights to share — you just have to ask!

Insights From a Media Relations Pro

When Chris Osborne was hired as the public relations manager for the Jefferson County (Ala.) Department of Public Health, he did what any seasoned media relations pro would do: He conducted an audit of the agency's past news coverage to understand the relationship the health department had with the media. Much to his surprise, Osborne realized he had a tough challenge ahead of him to improve relationships with local media.

Training the Executive Team en Masse

When I accepted a new position with a local government agency, one of my first tasks included researching the organization's subject matter experts (SMEs) and reviewing some of their past interviews. Much to my surprise, several versions of a "gotcha"-style exposé featuring my new employer — and even worse, my new CEO — jumped right out of my Google search. The organization has several divisions that include clinical and environmental as the primary functions. The troubling news stories I located involved our Environmental Division, which is comprised largely of engineers and inspectors.

One story I watched was the two-part environmental series, "Deadly Deceptions," that aired on the local CBS affiliate in Birmingham. The investigative report focused on allegations of failings in the federally mandated air program and subsequent air quality issues in a particular area of Jefferson County. I watched our stoic expert engineers using complicated terms and scientific language while addressing people who simply wanted answers they could understand and results they could see.

As if that was not challenging enough, the critical and highly promoted *"Tune in tonight at 10"* teaser featured our frustrated CEO pointing at the camera to get out of his space as he exited a contentious community meeting. The camera followed him as he walked to a nearby hallway water fountain (either to cool off or drown himself!). The result was a reporter following him and firing questions like an old western Gatlin Gun. I sat silently in my new office watching this video of these media catastrophes, and I cringed, realizing that media training had to be a top priority.

I met with my new public relations team and laid out the plan. Every manager, SME and executive needed to experience a comprehensive eight-hour media training session, and it had to be mandatory. This was no small feat, but with fresh wounds to the organization's reputation, the executive management team (EMT) agreed the training could be beneficial.

The overall sentiment from the training participants was that the media were evil and deliberately sought ways to make our organization look bad. Of course, years of missteps and ill-advised media encounters might make one (or in this case an entire organization) a little salty. I explained that while the media are not your friend, they don't have to be your foe. I provided classroom instruction of basic interviewing principles and best practices, followed by mock interviews featuring some of the top media talent in the market to make the scenarios as realistic as possible. The mock interviews were recorded for critique sessions.

(continued)

One by one, the participants entered and ran the gauntlet of mock media interviews, some broadcast, some print and some using cell phones. After private review with each individual and then a humbling peer review in a group setting, the layers of the onion had been peeled away.

What resulted is a new method of operation, now in its sixth year, of providing public information, sharing facts about innovative programs and embracing tough situations using the tools of transparency, preparation, honesty and expertise as leaders in our field. Many of our staff members now embrace our media partners, notice a change in the news stories' tone and invite the reporters to follow our initiatives.

The dividends from this investment in training have continued to pay off. During our most challenging period, the 2020 COVID-19 pandemic, not one negative story involving our organization lived beyond a single news cycle, which is a remarkable accomplishment.

ACTION STEPS

Complete the communication and media audits for your organization or client (or, if you are not working with an organization, conduct the audit for an issue or industry) to provide the research you need to move further with development of your media training plan.

A. Following the prompts, gather data on the stakeholders and media coverage for your organization or issue. Make the Action Steps work for your needs and learning goals — feel free to adjust the Action Steps as suggested in the directions.

B. Once you complete the audits, summarize your findings and draft a plan to share the results with the participants in your media relations training program.

CHAPTER FOUR ACTION STEPS: COMMUNICATION AND MEDIA AUDITS

Part A

Conduct a **communication audit** for your client, organization or issue. Revise the prompts as needed to customize the research for your particular industry, issue or organization type. Refer to the process for conducting communication audits in this chapter to complete the steps below.

1. **Identify the scope of the audit.** Who are your internal and external stakeholders?
2. **Gather samples for review.** What communication materials have you used in the past?
3. **Ask questions and collect feedback by using primary research.** What primary research will you use to gain insights from your key stakeholders?
4. **Determine strengths, weakness, opportunities and threats.** Using the data you collect, create your SWOT table.
5. **Conduct an analysis and consider recommendations.** Based on what you have learned, what are the current priorities for achieving your goals for media relations?

6. **Identify parts of your mission, vision and values that will drive *ethical decision-making* as you communicate with your key stakeholders.**

7. **Revisit your strategic plan.** What are three things you can include in your media relations strategy that will help establish or bolster your reputation with your most important media contacts?

Part B

Now that you have conducted the larger communication audit with your stakeholders, it's time to look more closely at your actual media coverage results. Conduct a **media audit** for your organization, your primary issue or industry, or both. Make these criteria work for your needs and learning goals — feel free to adjust them as needed. *Your instructor may have additional criteria for advanced courses.*

Suggested Criteria:

1. Data collection and analysis tools:
   a. This will depend on what you have available to you at your school or work. If you have no access to media monitoring tools, set up a research plan using Google News or other free online search engines to search for the key words you have identified. Your school or business may already have a subscription to a media monitoring service.
   b. Regardless of the tools you use, create a list of keywords that you will use in your search terms (e.g., your organization's name, words that describe an issue or industry, or even identifiers for an event such as a food recall or product announcement).
   c. Identify the pool of media sources you wish to review (may be regional, national, international, trade-specific, print only, Spanish broadcast — in other words, what is the primary market for your news?).

2. Timeframe: past 12 months (again, refine to suit your needs and get the snapshot that will be meaningful for your organization).

3. Analysis: Besides collecting descriptive statistics, you will want to evaluate the sentiment (positive, negative, neutral) and accuracy of the reporting. This will be done through systematic content analysis of the news stories, either manually or assisted by software applications.

Results:

1. Number of media hits in timeframe: _____

2. Top 5-10 media outlets by volume: _____
   a. Approximate reach (i.e., number of views of the news stories as well as geographic areas. Many media monitoring services also can provide valuable demographics on the readers/viewers of the media outlets.) _____
   b. Sentiment results (with examples). _____
   c. Accuracy results (with examples)._____

3. Executive Summary: How is your organization faring in media coverage? Who are your friends and anti-friends in the media industry? Are you reaching your key publics in these media channels? Can you identify key media outlets that you need to focus your future media relations efforts on? What can you do to improve how you and your spokespeople tell the story? Any additional insights? _____

Part C

With your audit results and executive summary in hand, work with your media relations team to develop ways to incorporate this data into your training program. List at least three things you can do to help your training participants better understand the media climate they will be operating in. Refer to the reading for more ideas for sharing the results.

NOTES

[1] The full report is available from https://www.edelman.com/trust/2020-trust-barometer/

[2] William A. Galston, "Is Seeing Still Believing? The Deepfake Challenge to Truth in Politics," Brookings Institution, January 8, 2020. Available at http://www.brookings.edu/research/is-seeing-still-believing-the-deepfake-challenge-to-truth-in-politics/

[3] Sample external communication audit questions can be found on the SoGo Survey Blog located at https://www.sogosurvey.com/blog/5-key-questions-for-your-external-communication-audit/

[4] The first-known use of the acronym S.M.A.R.T. is in George T. Doran, "There's a S.M.A.R.T. Way to Write Management's Goals and Objectives." *Management Review* 70(11) (Nov. 1981): 35.

[5] For a comprehensive review of the plethora of media monitoring services available, read Matias Rodsevich, "50 Best Media Monitoring Tools for News and Social Media," PRLab. Available at https://prlab.co/the-best-50-media-monitoring-tools-for-news-and-social-media/

[6] For more on measurement and evaluation, see Chapter 10 of Howard, Mathews, and Horsley, *On Deadline: Managing Media Relations*, 6th ed.(Waveland Press, 2021).

Picking the Team

AGENDA

1. Learn the various roles that will create a strong media relations team for your organization.
2. Understand why you need policies for who speaks to the media on which topics.
3. Develop a plan to train all the members of your team.
4. Recognize the value of including external experts for your media relations team.
5. Complete the Action Steps at the end of the chapter.

KEY CONCEPTS

Spokesperson
Subject Matter Expert (SME)
Third-Party Verifier

Who's Up To Bat and Who's on Deck?

There's been quite a bit of discussion about building trust and the development of relationships with stakeholders as part of your organization's communication mission. You've gone through a great deal of effort to create a plan and compelling messaging that tells your organization's story while motivating your target audience to action. Now it's time to identify, recruit and prepare the teammates that you'll rely on to deliver the organization's story during normal business operations and, even more important, during a crisis. The ability (or inability) of a **spokesperson** or **subject matter expert (SME)** to deliver the organization's message can make or break a business situation, affecting the level of trust in relationships with key stakeholders.

This chapter is designed to help you, the media relations professional, think through why you need to identify a spokesperson(s) for your organization. You will learn why the company's designated spokesperson is not always the best person to speak for the organization; when an SME should be used; what traits are most desirable in a spokesperson/SME, and what traits to avoid; what is expected of a spokesperson; how to develop a spokesperson and a subject matter expert; and when it is acceptable to include partners outside your organization to speak on your behalf. As you identify and establish your spokesperson and SME team roster, you must be confident that they will knock the message delivery out of the park, especially during the bottom of the ninth inning.

Who's Doing the Talking?

Every organization has a person or a team of people who are tasked to be "the face" or the public representative of the organization. These individuals are called

NPR correspondent Elissa Nadworny interviewed Tony Chaffin, an instructor of building construction technology at Texas State Technical College, in March 2022 for a story on career opportunities for graduates. The TSTC communication director worked with Chaffin in advance to prepare him for his role as a subject matter expert in this national radio broadcast interview. **PHOTO CREDIT: PETER MACÍAS.**

upon to deliver information about the company — new products and services, corporate financials, human interest stories, and vital information during a crisis. Essentially, the spokesperson and SMEs are the conduit to the public through media reports.

If you think about it, there's not a shred of information that a professional communicator shares with stakeholders that doesn't impact people. The media choose stories that they want to report on because they will have an impact on their audiences. It is for that reason that having a spokesperson(s) is so important. It's the human connection between the public and the organization. It lets the public know that the organization is not just a logo but an entity being run by people who are willing to share information that could impact the local, regional and global community.

Insights From a Media Relations Pro

How do you know when to use an organizational spokesperson or a subject matter expert? Lawrence Wells, former bureau chief (ABC News) and supervising producer (NBC News) describes the differences between these important roles from a news professional's perspective.

The Vital Roles of Spokesperson and Subject Matter Expert

A *spokesperson* is the outward facing (public) representative of your organization. This person is the public representation of who your organization is and what it stands for. They should be comfortable delivering your organization's message with confidence and communicate accurately across the airwaves or in print, all while being clear and presenting a positive demeanor. They should be able to answer questions, but, most important, if they don't know the answer or are unsure of the answer, they should say so and promise to clarify before the end of the day.

Subject matter experts are critical parts of the information chain. They know the subject better, and in greater depth, than anyone else. The more technical the information, the more difficult it is to explain accurately to the nonexpert. The ability to explain technical or complicated issues clearly is critical to the role of an SME.

The SME can be used to further explain issues to the public and/or brief the spokesperson to assure accuracy. In the reporting world, spokespersons are viewed differently. The spokesperson, to a reporter who has had experience with a wide variety of spokespersons, is the person who delivers the official version of events; that is, they may be delivering an accurate but not wholly revealing version of events.

The SME is often a source to a reporter. I have — at various times — had SMEs in fields as varied as organized crime, nuclear engineering, aerospace engineering, arson, construction, drug smuggling, constitutional law and Lebanese politics. They could — and sometimes did — go on camera to further explain or reinforce points the reporter was making. Most of the time they provided essential information and explanations to the producer and reporter to make complex subjects clear.

More important, SMEs sometimes help direct reporters and news producers to critical information that reveals the larger story. For example, a source of mine who worked on a committee staff on Capitol Hill not only explained the inner workings of nuclear reactors to me, but he directed me to other experts aware of failings at U.S. reactors. That person's guidance — and our reporting — led to a federal investigation that shut down the Tennessee Valley Authority for 18 months while flaws in their construction and safety programs were identified and corrected.

(continued)

There is no greater challenge for public relations/media relations professionals than having to disclose bad news. That news can be anything: a scandal, pharmaceutical contamination or sabotage, a drop in stock values, accidental injury or death — notably as a result of negligence, professional malpractice or illegal activities of any kind. The list is long. The lack of transparency or the attempt to push inaccurate information is a cause for a news agency to take a closer look into the situation or story, which could spell disaster for your organization.

Thus the earlier that board members, management or the media get bad news, the easier it is to address. Covering up information inevitably ends up in worse results than honest disclosure. The credibility of the organization is at stake. Nowhere is this more obvious than in the media.

For more than 20 years I worked as a network news producer and reporter (at the network, a reporter is different from a correspondent). I was involved in investigations involving members of Congress, drug smuggling, corporate malfeasance, negligence by federal agencies, plane crashes, civil rights bombings, arson, money laundering by labor unions, and more. In nearly every case, a public relations spokesperson helped trigger or expand the investigation by saying the wrong thing.

Remember Sean Spicer with his inaccurate statement that the Trump Inauguration drew the largest crowds in U.S. history? Spicer was useless as a spokesperson after that single incident. His credibility was gone. So was that of the White House. The result? Every statement issued by the White House was fact-checked by the major media, resulting in uncovering over 30,500 deliberate misstatements over four years. For this reason, each and every member of your organization's spokesperson and SME cadre should be vetted and trained before stepping up to the microphone to speak on behalf of your organization.

Likewise, too careful a denial can trigger a closer look: Did the parties meet on Tuesday? No, they did not (it was a Wednesday). Is there any evidence that XYZ had been drinking before the accident? No, there isn't (XYZ was not given a timely breathalyzer). There has never been any reason to believe this piece of equipment had any kind of weakness (until we found the 8-year-old warning bulletin from the federal regulator detailing the specific weakness).

These denials — once revealed — paint the spokesperson and the entire organization as being without credibility. At that point, the media can become a swarm of insects delivering death by a thousand stings.

Keep in mind that the organization's usual spokesperson (e.g., a member of the media relations team or someone from the marketing department) may not always be the best person to deliver the company's messaging, and there are a number of factors in which the professional communicator may need to find an alternate person. One example may be when an organization finds itself in a crisis. To mitigate the impact of the crisis and to ensure a solid relationship with internal and external stakeholders, it may be appropriate to call upon a member of the leadership team (chairman of the board, CEO or COO). The executive can assure stakeholders that all is safe, the crisis is being resolved and steps are being taken to ensure this crisis will never happen again. The executive may also explain where stakeholders who are affected by the crisis can go to get assistance. In this situation the leader serving as spokesperson may be delivering the exact same message that the organization's usual spokesperson would, but the leader will be viewed by the public as someone with decision-making authority working to resolve the crisis.

Another example of an alternate to the organization's dedicated spokesperson is a person who is not affiliated with the organization but can provide a third-party testimonial to quality, effectiveness, convenience and impact of a product or service. This type of spokesperson's message delivery can be a very powerful tool when trying to convince stakeholders of the efficacy of the company's products or services.

Developing a Training Plan

We know you've heard the phrase "practice makes perfect." The same goes for the development of spokespersons and SMEs. Once you've identified the people who will make up your spokesperson/SME roster, it's time to train them. There are many ways to train your team, but the one we've found most successful is developing tabletop exercises based on a particular scenario. This will take an extended amount of time on your part as the trainer and facilitator. We provide a more in-depth discussion of training in Chapter 11, but the following is a basic guide for a tabletop exercise:

1. Identify a date and time for the exercise that fits participants' schedules.
2. Create a realistic scenario based upon actual issues, plans or activities in your organization.
3. Develop and provide supporting documents for the trainee to use, such as:
   a. Talking points to ensure the accuracy of information about to be provided by the subject matter experts (see Chapter 8).
   b. Frequently asked questions (FAQs).
   c. Preparation checklist (see Chapter 12).
   d. List of potential questions they may be asked by the reporter.
4. Help trainees prepare for a media interview. They must:
   a. Know what they're going to say and how to say it.
   b. Understand how to conduct a television, radio, print, online publication or podcast interview.
   c. Anticipate the types of questions a reporter may ask and how to answer them.
   d. Practice critically listening to a reporter's questions to avoid a pitfall.
   e. Become aware of their body language and movement during interviews.
   f. Learn how the organization's professional communicator will support them.
5. Establish what criteria you'll use to evaluate the trainees. It could include:
   a. Ability to accurately deliver the company's message.
   b. On-camera presence, tone and body language.

    c. Ability to answer reporter's questions while not straying from their talking points.

    d. Professional demeanor that demonstrates the ability to stay calm and focused.

6. Identify other communication professionals to help conduct the performance evaluation of the participants.

7. Set up time to conduct individual/in-person reviews after their training session.

All this training does three important things: First, it helps you distinguish which teammates you will use as your varsity squad and which teammates will serve as backup. Second, it provides your spokespersons/SMEs with a view into the challenges of media relations and an understanding of how important it is to execute the communication mission. Third, it will identify teammates who *think* they can serve as spokespersons/SMEs but find that this responsibility is further out of their comfort zone than they expected.

Here's an important note on suitability of team members: Cultivating spokesperson/SME team members is a long-term process. Don't completely reject a teammate who's decided that being in front of the camera or a mic is not for them, because they can still make a difference. Encourage these teammates to assist you with generating answers to media questions and submitting them in writing. It keeps them engaged, provides you with direct access to expert knowledge, allows the SME to get some credit in the news story for their contribution and encourages them to continue with their spokesperson/SME role.

Insights From a Media Relations Pro

Not all spokespersons are created equal, as each has a distinct personality and style. That includes you. As the organization's media relations professional, how will you decide who will be the forward-facing spokesperson? Jeanne Hamrick, director of communications at North American Securities Administrators Association, is a top communication professional with a keen ability to identify and train quality spokesperson teams. Here she shares what she looks for in a great spokesperson.

Traits to Consider When Choosing a Spokesperson

The role of a spokesperson is vital to any organization's success. As the public face of the business, the communications strategy used by a spokesperson reflects not only its executive leadership but the entity's shareholders, products, employees and reputation. Your expertise as the media relations professional will be essential in choosing the best spokesperson for each type of interview.

Confidence and competence are apparent. The best path toward these objectives in one's role as a spokesperson is to be prepared. They should rehearse for media interviews for print, podcasts, radio, TV, the internet and social media by developing and sticking to key messages that they want to deliver. They will practice responding to hostile or "softball" questions with answers that don't reflect badly on the journalist or your organization. Also, consider asking a journalist for questions that you can share with the spokesperson in advance of the interview.

(continued)

Don't be surprised or offended if they refuse. Afterward, follow up with the journalist to answer any additional questions and to ensure article and quote accuracy.

As an organization's gatekeeper, you hold its reputation in your hands and must carefully choose the most appropriate spokesperson for the subject matter. The spokesperson must be an engaging speaker and an effective storyteller with deep and wide knowledge of your employer. They should be mindful of the accuracy and the effect of their words. They should ensure messaging does not offend any individual, group or audience. The communication profession evolves, but truth in communication is steadfast and paramount. If they don't have facts, it is better to wait, reschedule a deadline and get back to a journalist with the accurate information than to give an inaccurate statement that would force cleanup afterward.

As the media relations professional for your organization, it is essential that you take the initiative to find new or creative solutions to pitch story ideas to journalists or influencers. They may not reach out to you initially, so create a list of media influencers, introduce yourself to each one and then pitch them a story. Seize upon the opportunity to pitch an influencer even it if is to say that a big announcement is coming down the road. Reach out to journalists on background to share details in advance so they have time to write an accurate article. Be prepared by creating holding statements for media situations that could affect the company's reputation in the case of worse case scenarios. Consider all possible disaster scenarios ahead of time, which means less time spent drafting messaging and cleaning up when bad things happen. If they do happen, get out and get ahead of them as quickly as you can.

Develop positive relationships with external audiences — journalists and influencers — and with internal audiences such as members of the board of directors, company leadership and staff members. All are key sources to ensure message accuracy. External audiences including journalists, government officials or regulators, competitors and social media bloggers or writers can affect the target audience's perception and the reputation of your company. The more networking you do now, the more potential allies you will have. You must have multifaceted relationships as the media's response to and perception of the company will drive the success of you and your spokesperson.

Including External Partners on Your Media Relations Team

When it comes to telling your organization's story, the spokesperson/SME is expected to step up and provide quality, accurate and timely information regarding an event, product/service or crisis. But there may come a time when your organization finds itself in a situation that requires the backing of an outside entity or source to serve as a verifier — a third-party testimonial.

"A **third-party verifier** can be a powerful spokesperson/SME for your organization," said Jonathan Aiken, former anchor for CNN and former national spokesperson for the National Office of the American Red Cross. "There is a natural tendency to view an outside source as more truthful. Using a third-party verifier can solidify credibility, strengthen trust, help mitigate the sting of a crisis and make a positive impact for your organization with your target audiences."

Aiken shared a number of things to consider before using an outside spokesperson:

1. Take time to identify and create a list of possible outside spokespersons/ subject matter experts.
2. Invite them to join the organization's formal spokesperson training. If the training doesn't fit their schedule, offer to sit with them one-on-one and go over the upcoming interview.
3. Coordinate messaging and be crystal clear regarding what should and should not be said (spokesperson training for the external partner is helpful for this).
4. Understand the risk versus reward for using a third-party verifier. Consider using a third-party verifier only when necessary and for specific target audiences. A downfall of using an outside spokesperson too often is the possibility that your stakeholders will perceive your organization as incapable of conveying its own message and thereby opening you up for more intense scrutiny.

For an example of effective use of a third-party verifier, consider the case of statewide sales tax holidays for back-to-school shopping. Many states that have a sales tax will temporarily suspend collecting taxes on items that are considered essential for returning to school, such as clothes, uniforms and school supplies. It seems like a great opportunity for stores of all types, from big box stores to local mom and pop shops, to promote their goods for the sales tax holiday, right? However, this can backfire if shoppers sense the businesses are only participating for their own gains, or they may even be secretly inflating prices to take advantage of shoppers who believe they can find bargains.

How would you address your company's credibility to encourage shoppers during the sales tax holiday? One option may be to invite an official from a local school district to explain how the sales tax holiday works and to ensure shoppers that they can save money by buying back-to-school items during that time period. Another may be to invite a leader from a nonprofit that supports education to participate in an interview from their store and demonstrate which items will be excluded from taxes. Be creative when thinking about which external partners can be a valuable source of credibility for your organization.

ACTION STEPS

You've done your research, developed your philosophy and convinced your organization's leadership that they should support your media relations training efforts. Now it's time to take a closer look at your personnel and start determining who would make the best spokespersons and SMEs to support your organization's mission, vision and values.

Complete the Action Steps for this chapter. Working with your team, analyze the strengths and weaknesses that you identified in Chapter 1's Action Steps to generate your plan for using spokespersons and SMEs.

CHAPTER FIVE ACTION STEPS:
CHOOSING YOUR SPOKESPERSONS AND SMEs

Part A

Take a critical look at your team members to determine who would be the best fit as spokespersons or SMEs. If you are still missing key people, brainstorm who else in the organization should be added to your team.

1. According to your assessment results in Chapter 1, who would you consider to be ready to serve as a spokesperson or an SME? Do you need to approach other members of your organization to serve in these roles? _____

2. Give an example of when a spokesperson might not be the best person to deliver your organization's or client's message. _____

3. When choosing your organization's spokesperson, what traits are you looking for? In other words, what specific knowledge or characteristics are required to represent your particular organization? _____

4. Do all members of your organization's leadership team have the qualifications or experience to serve as a spokesperson or a subject matter expert when necessary? If not, how would you approach providing a training program for them? _____

Part B

Now consider what it would be like to work with an outside partner on your media relations training. Describe a situation in which you might use a third-party verifier as a spokesperson or SME for your organization. Is there someone your organization has partnered with in the past? What would be your concerns when working with an external partner in your particular line of business? What would be the greatest benefit?

Resources for a Successful Media Training Experience

AGENDA

1. Learn what technology and other resources are needed to support a successful and effective media relations training program.

2. Understand the benefits of and what is needed for training with video conference platforms.

3. Learn how to take an inventory of your current resources, create a list of the essential items you are missing and add a wish list of items that will elevate your media training efforts.

4. Think strategically about your approach to gaining leadership's approval for your budget and to developing partnerships for sharing and borrowing resources.

5. Complete the Action Steps at the end of the chapter.

KEY CONCEPTS

Training Resources

Training Equipment

Training Personnel

Scalable Media Training Resources

Return on Investment (ROI)

Realistic Training Is a Must for Today's Media Environment

You wouldn't expect a professional basketball player to train without a basketball, an ice skater to train without ice skates or an equestrian to train without a horse. Likewise, media trainers need the right equipment to create realistic training situations that allow the learner to become comfortable with all the gadgets used by modern journalists.

Whether you are creating a media relations training program for a class or for your business, you eventually need the right tools to conduct effective and realistic training sessions for your team. While this may sound expensive and out of reach at first, the good news is that some strategic thinking can enable you to procure the resources you need, with your leadership's support and with a bottom line that fits your budget.

For this chapter we consulted with Laura Howe, senior vice president of Global Corporate Communications for Pearson PLC, a provider of educational materials and learning technologies.[1] Howe has experience developing media training programs for nonprofits and global corporations, and she shared her recommendations for getting the right equipment without blowing your budget.

How to Determine Your Resource Needs

When it comes to creating your list of media training resources, don't try to mimic other organizations' inventories just because they seem to have exactly what *they* need. The real question is, what do *you* need?

Howe encourages media trainers to start with questions "that will determine what you need but also determine how to get people to buy into that and provide you with some of those resources: What am I trying to accomplish with this? What kind of training do I need to put in place?" Those questions will more than likely point back to your organization's communication strategic plan; no media plan should be developed unless you already have goals, objectives, strategies and tactics for your overall communication endeavors (as described in Chapter 2).[2]

Every organization has its own approach to media relations and uses for earned media (unpaid media coverage of an organization by third parties) that are based upon its mission. Determine if your organization's media relations activities require trained spokespersons for *regular media interactions*, preparation of subject matter experts to present *technical information* or building a team for *crisis or emergency responses*, or situational training for *occasional one-on-one interviews*. Understanding the situation(s) and extent to which you need to engage with media will help you shape a training program that is best suited for your organization's mission without unnecessary resource expenditures.

The Right Equipment and Personnel for the Job

Once you have a full understanding of your media relations goals, you can start gathering your **training resources.** As Howe explains, each of the above scenarios requires training for a specific set of skills and requires **training equipment** and **training personnel.** Also keep in mind the ability to scale up or down, depending upon your organization's current situation; your equipment may vary from a smartphone and tripod with a simple light kit and mic to a large setup with full-size cameras and lights.

A realistic training environment that imitates the scenario and the media engagement experience will provide long-lasting learning for your team. This environment includes cameras, lights and the personnel to run them, as well as the ability to play back interviews for instant critiques. It is vital for people to see their own performance to fully understand what went well and what needs work. While it can be painful and unnatural for trainees to watch their interview attempts, it is key to help people see how they appear on camera and what they sound like while responding to reporters' questions.

Once you have the equipment and the knowledge of your media outlets, you need experts to guide you through the training experience. This includes at least two

Laura Howe, a communication executive for a global academic publisher, played the role of a reporter in a media training exercise for public relations students at The University of Alabama in April 2022. The cameras, lavalier mics, camera operators and lighting in the campus television studio added to the realism of this exercise, in which students served as spokespersons for their class client.
Photo credit: J. Suzanne Horsley.

"reporters," one who can run the interview and focus on the content of your trainees' answers while the other focuses on their nonverbals, such as body movement, use of hands, eye direction, facial expressions and even voice inflections. These reporters may be colleagues, others within your school or organization who are experienced at media relations or external resources such as hired consultants or former journalists.

Whether you need an entry training setup or a highly professional, realistic one, you still need qualified training personnel who will elevate the professionalism and reality of the scenario while providing honest, helpful critiques of the participants. These personnel include coaches, camera/sound operators, reporters, evaluators and technical experts. Depending upon the goals for the training session, the training staff may be all internal employees who have sufficient media experience, or the staff may include external consultants who can help your team develop the skill level needed for crises, emergencies or other highly public activities. In addition, feedback coming from an external consultant, as opposed to a colleague, is often better received because the participants are not as inclined to take that criticism personally. Figure 6.1 "Inventory for **scalable media training resources**," provides a guide that adapts to the training scenario your team needs.

It's also important to note that scenario-based training will not be helpful if you and your team are not avid, daily consumers of the news. You will not have an informed sense of what is or is not effective if you don't watch cable and network broadcasts, listen to news radio or read published interviews in print or online newspapers and magazines. Regular consumption and critical examinations of media coverage will make you and your team much better prepared to work with news professionals. It will also help you develop the most relevant media list, as we discussed in Chapter 4.

Training With Video Conferencing Platforms Is Essential

Video conferencing platforms, such as Skype, Zoom and Google Meet, became ubiquitous during the COVID-19 pandemic, and they are here to stay. This technology has made it easier for budget-strapped media outlets to get more news material with fewer staff and resources, and it has also made it more efficient for media relations pros to have access to media outlets from around the globe. Therefore, it is important to include both face-to-face and video conference interview formats in your media training planning.

The technology to play back the recorded interviews is more affordable than ever and doesn't require a high level of technological skill. Howe conducts regular mock interviews for her company's CEO over video conferencing platforms and plays back the recordings instantly. Others watch the practice session from behind the scenes to give feedback as soon as the mock interview ends. She says this format saves time, especially for busy CEOs who have limited time to devote to training before moving on to other matters. If you are hiring consultants for your training on a tight budget, this can minimize the number of hours you are paying for their expertise.

Materials	Personnel
Entry Level Cost: About $1,000-$2,000 depending upon the electronic devices you already have.	
Recording device • Smartphone or basic/consumer quality digital camera. Tripod • Desk type or telescopic floor tripod. Light kit • Sized to accommodate a single speaker. External mic • Inexpensive wired lavalier (lapel) microphones (greatly enhances the audio and reduces background noise). Earphones • Ear buds or headsets to replicate remote interviews with radio or television outlets. Computer or laptop • To play videos or to practice using video conferencing software (such as Zoom or Skype).	Training at this level is possible with two people who role-play as a reporter and a camera operator and with an evaluator who observes and gives feedback. The trainers may be internal staff or external consultants and should have moderate to high levels of experience in media interviews, either as a spokesperson or a journalist. This level of training is appropriate for routine interviews, special topic interviews (like product launches or events) and subject matter expert training.
Professional Level for Realistic Training Cost: Varies widely. For intense media interview training, this level can replicate all media environments from routine to crisis.	
All the above resources: • These basic items should be owned by the organization and readily available to those needing training or periodic refreshers. Do not rely on personally owned electronic devices for this level of training. Additional rented, owned or shared resources: • High-quality cameras, lights, microphones, IFB system. • Green screens or backgrounds to enhance the realism. • For press conference training, a room with a podium or speaker's table and seating or standing area for reporters. • Devices and software to record the interviews and provide instant playback on computers and monitors; private online video channels such as YouTube or Vimeo to share videos with participants.	Training at this level requires external consultants or highly experienced internal staff (either from your department or elsewhere in the organization). The number will vary depending upon how many individuals are going through the training. At a minimum, realistic training sessions require a coach for the interviewee(s), a reporter, a camera and a sound operator, an evaluator and a technical expert to set up the equipment and monitor the recordings and playback. The budget should allow for hiring media training consultants or working journalists who will enhance the realism of the training experience. This level of training is appropriate for the types of interviews listed in "How To Determine Your Resource Needs," as well as for crisis or emergency response interviews, press conferences, highly technical subject matter expert interviews, media tours, major product launches and other significant organizational announcements, such as mergers or layoffs.

(continued)

FIGURE 6.1   Inventory for scalable media training resources.

Materials	Personnel
Moderate Level Teams and organizations may need a mix of the entry level and professional level resources when they seldom engage in media relations activities or only need training for specific, singular activities.	
Equipment and pricing will vary based up on the specific goals of the training and the types of media interaction.	If your organization does not engage often with media, or your staff or subject matter experts rarely do interviews, trainers should be highly skilled experts who can provide meaningful training experiences to prepare the speakers for these episodic interviews.

FIGURE 6.1   Inventory for scalable media training resources (cont.).

However, just because you are participating in an online interview doesn't mean that you don't put the same, if not more, thought into how to train for this format. As we will discuss in Chapter 9, you need to train with the same equipment and in the same environment in which you would conduct the interview. When you play back the interviews during your training critique session, also examine the quality of the lighting, sound and visual content. Follow the checklist on p. 51 to plan your equipment budget for video conference interview training.

Earning Leadership Support for Your Training Budget

The best way to initiate a conversation about your media training budget with organizational leadership is first to connect the objectives of your media training plan from Chapter 2 to the broader strategic plan. Media training should never be done in a vacuum and must be connected to organizational priorities; articulating this connection for executives will help them see the value in the investment. Just as your organization's strategic plan is proactive, your leaders will see the benefit in proactive media relations efforts. Howe explains that this approach creates a stronger argument for your budget because it feels more like a broad strategy and less like a one-off event with little return for the up-front expenses. Remind executives that the people being trained for media are also benefitting in other ways, such as in their public speaking, presentation and internal communication skills.

The second step is to determine what other activities or departments you can tie in with this investment of resources. Your case will be stronger if you demonstrate that the equipment and personnel can also benefit other organizational departments. For example, you can explain how you will share the resources with other departments such as human resources to create training videos. Marketing and social media teams can use the same equipment to create content, and they may also have personnel who can help your training efforts with their knowledge of your organization's background, products and services. Advertising and in-house creative teams may already have some of the equipment you need, or they may be willing to do cost sharing with your department. Prepare a list of all departments in your organization

Checklist: Equipment for Video Conference Interviews

✓ **Branded or recognizable background.** The background needs to identify the entity you are representing in your interview. This may be as simple as a logo or sign on a wall, or a recognizable symbol such as a distinctive architectural feature at your university or corporate headquarters. However, to ensure easy identification without concerns about lighting, noise or other distractions, invest in a *step-and-repeat backdrop* that features your logo and trademark printed on a fabric or paper screen. Purchasing a portable backdrop that is large enough for seated, standing and group shots makes this a multipurpose investment that will serve your organization for many years (or, at least until the organization changes its branding). Use your chosen backdrop for all training sessions to ensure that it works for video and to get your team used to posing in front of it. A note of caution: Do not use the digital background options provided by the video conference platforms. These can distort the spokesperson's image and be a distraction for the viewer when hair or body parts blend into the digitized background.

✓ **Good lighting.** Invest in good lighting equipment that will reduce shadows on the speaker's face while also showing off your chosen backdrop. *Ring lights* are now ubiquitous and affordable, and they provide perfect lighting for video interviews. These lights come in a variety of sizes from freestanding on a tripod to a desktop version with a holder for a smartphone. Purchase the size and style that you will get the most use from to help you stay within budget.

✓ **Sound equipment.** For online videos, less is more when it comes to equipment that is visible in the shot. Invest in a *lavalier mic* with a long cord (10 feet or longer) that can be used for on-camera standup interviews as well as sit-down video conferencing. These clip onto the spokesperson's collar with minimal visual interference and will have better sound quality than that of the built-in mic on a laptop or mobile device. You can also use wireless ear buds if you find, during your practice sessions, that they provide good sound quality. Earphones used with a chin mic or a large radio-style microphone that is visible on camera can appear bulky and distracting — does it make sense for your company image to have this type of equipment on view? Perhaps it would for podcasters or radio personalities, but not so much for company executives. Consider the visual impact of all devices that will be visible in the camera shot.

✓ **Computers or mobile devices.** Always conduct your training on the same equipment you will use for the interview. If you anticipate most interviews will be done from the office, use a computer with Ethernet cables or strong, secure and reliable wireless connections. If you do most interviews from the field or other remote locations, practice on smartphones or tablets with reliable hot spot connections and get a tripod for stability — don't rely on someone to hold the device.

that could potentially share the costs of equipment with your media relations team. There are multiple potential uses for everything in your media training toolbox.

College students can often get all the equipment they need for their class's media relations training from their school's library or digital media lab, local television news outlets or community nonprofits. Reach out to the media and PR professionals in your community for assistance in getting loaned equipment or trainers for your team. Pros are usually eager to share their time and talents with students and can often get leave time from their jobs to volunteer.

Students aren't the only ones who can benefit from community resources; pros can also seek loaned equipment from public libraries and partner with other professionals to share resources and training opportunities. Networking and developing professional relationships will benefit your media relations team in more ways than one.

Demonstrating Return on Investment

Once you have the resources secured for your equipment and personnel, it's important to demonstrate the **return on investment (ROI)** to leadership so that they will continue to support your team's efforts in the future. However, it can be difficult to show ROI for training, just as it is challenging to show ROI for any public relations work. Showcase your team's successes by sharing examples of good media interviews, reports of media coverage and any changes in the number of media inquiries your department receives. Highlight media clips featuring spokespersons and subject matter experts who completed the training. Remember to feature effective examples in your next media training sessions.

Find ways to connect revenue streams (sales of products or services, fundraising, audience attendance, etc.) to media coverage that supported these programs. Look for positive changes in your ongoing customer approval ratings or for other measures of organizational success that occurred after media-trained spokespersons conducted interviews. Of course, if there are negative changes, use that feedback to improve your training program. Finally, evaluate the media appearances themselves: create a rubric to measure message accuracy, spokesperson delivery and the value of the media outlet to demonstrate to your executives how effective the media training has been. Take all your measures and relate them to specific objectives in your organization's strategic plan when presenting your reports, on either a monthly or a quarterly basis.

Cameras, Lights, Messaging!

Cameras, lighting and instant playback are worthless if your participants don't have a grasp of the key messages and talking points for the practice interviews. Whether you are in a classroom or a corporate headquarters, the media training will have no value if the participants are not part of a realistic scenario or if they are relegated to making up facts as they go. The messaging should be developed ahead of time and shared with all participants, including the trainers.

As Howe explains, once the participants are comfortable with the key messages, "the interview techniques will follow because you have the information you need to communicate." Regardless of the type of scenario you are training for (routine, crisis, special event, etc.), the participants need real facts and real equipment to benefit from the training sessions. This will allow them to walk away from the media training experience with more confidence to engage with reporters on behalf of their organization. Take the messaging you develop in Chapter 8 to create realistic scenarios and talking points for your training sessions.

Final Thoughts on Resources

While the equipment we've discussed in this chapter is important for a realistic, well-rounded training experience, it is certainly not required to learn how to do media interviews. With experienced trainers, willing participants and a little creativity, you can have a successful learning experience that will support your organization's media relations goals.

ACTION STEPS

Determine what your team really needs to put your organization's media relations philosophy and planning into action. Not every team needs a "professional level" of training, nor does every team need to spend thousands of dollars to achieve its goals.

Complete the Action Steps for this chapter by filling in the inventory of media training resources form for your desired level of media training and then by identifying strategies to obtain the resources you are missing.

1. Take your current inventory of media relations training equipment.
2. Determine what you need to get to successfully achieve your media relations goals.
3. Develop a budget to purchase or rent resources and identify strategies to share/borrow resources from within your school or organization or from professional partners in your field.

CHAPTER SIX ACTION STEPS: MEDIA RELATIONS TRAINING RESOURCE INVENTORY

Part A

Take your *current inventory* of media relations training equipment, based upon the "inventory for scalable media training resources" on pp. 49-50. Choose the level (entry, professional, or moderate) that would help your organization achieve the goals you outlined in Chapter 2, and then complete the "materials" and "personnel" columns, identifying the equipment and personnel you already have available. Add as many lines to the table as you need.

Materials	Personnel
What equipment do you already own or have ready access to?	Who already works for your organization or is otherwise available to your team to provide training?

Part B

Now that you have taken an inventory of your current resources, what is missing? Determine what you still need to successfully achieve your media relations goals based upon the level you selected and your goals for media relations training. Add as many lines to the table as you need.

Materials	Personnel
What equipment are you missing that is essential to achieving your goals?	What additional personnel do you need to achieve your desired level of media relations training?

Part C

Estimate your budget and develop strategies to share/borrow resources from within your organization or from partners in your field, or to obtain funding to purchase or rent new resources. Add as many lines to the table as you need.

Materials	Personnel
Internal: List other departments or programs in your school, workplace or professional network that have the equipment you wish to share or borrow.	**Internal:** List other departments or programs in your school, workplace or professional network that have the skilled personnel who can provide training.
Budget Justification: Develop a cost estimate and list of strategies to obtain funding to purchase or rent the equipment that you cannot access in any other way.	**Budget Justification:** Develop a cost estimate and list of strategies to obtain funding to hire consultants who can provide training for your team.
Costs:	Costs:
Purchasing Sources:	Potential Consultants:
Strategies:	Strategies:

NOTES

[1] Conversation and emails with J. Suzanne Horsley, June 2021.

[2] For more on strategic plans, also see Chapter 1 of Howard, Mathews, & Horsley, *On Deadline: Managing Media Relations*, 6th ed. (Waveland Press, 2021).

Planning for a Crisis

AGENDA

1. Understand what constitutes a crisis for your organization.
2. Recognize how crisis media relations is different from routine media relations.
3. Know the steps you must take when faced with a crisis.
4. Learn how to operate in a crisis command center and a joint information center.
5. Develop your plan for crisis media training and identify who should attend.
6. Complete the Action Steps at the end of the chapter.

KEY CONCEPTS

Crisis Media Relations
Crisis Media Relations Collateral
Crisis Command Center
Joint Information Center

Crisis Media Training Isn't Just for Disasters

One must admire the U.S. Coast Guard motto, *Semper Paratus* (Always Ready) and its impact on the Coast Guard's multifaceted mission. They administer our nation's maritime laws on the sea, conduct vital lifesaving missions, protect the U.S. marine environment and protect our country's coastline and ports. The Coast Guard is in a constant state of preparedness for when they are called into action. Semper Paratus is not just an ethereal phrase, it is the anchor point for a lifestyle and a mission of the people who serve in one of our nation's most important first responder organizations. What does this have to do with crisis communication?

While we expect organizations like the Coast Guard to prepare for crises, *any* organization can find itself in a situation that adversely affects its normal everyday operations. In this chapter we will delve deeper into media relations training for your team and why this is essential for conducting an effective crisis communication response.

The Crisis

Everything in your organization seems to be going well: Operations are running smoothly, products are being produced, service is being delivered, the team seems happy and your stakeholders seem satisfied. Suddenly, a situation strikes that knocks the organization off its daily routine and has the potential to impact the company in a negative fashion. The loss of trust with the community and damage to the organization's brand can have an immediate negative impact on the company's bottom line. It's a crisis.

A crisis can manifest in many ways:

- A breakdown in the manufacturing process.
- An accident at your facility that could cause harm to the surrounding community.
- A disruption in service delivery.
- An unhappy client who airs their concerns on social media.
- A disgruntled employee who has revealed your organization's proprietary manufacturing techniques to the public.
- A natural disaster that brings your business to a standstill.
- A member of your team under investigation by a law enforcement agency.
- A death on the production line.

To make matters worse, the media are calling and asking questions about the crisis situation. They want answers to "what's happening" and "what is your organization doing in response" and "how will your organization resolve the situation." To position you and your team for success and manage the onslaught of public scrutiny, you'll launch the organization's crisis communication plan and contact your spokesperson team to have them on standby for action.

Not Your Normal Work Routine

What makes **crisis media relations** different from your routine media relations? It's likely that your normal media relations day is filled with researching and creating new ways to capture your key publics' attention. You focus on communicating the great things your organization is doing and how its products or services add value to your target audience's lives. You're using your best storytelling capabilities that answer the who, what, when, where, why and how questions. By combining the answers to those questions, you're creating a robust narrative with human interest, solid details and relevancy that ultimately capture your target audience's interest to make them care about what you have to say.

But now the day has gone off the rails; something has caused a significant interruption in your daily routine, and now you have to refocus how you're going to conduct your media relations work. The phone is ringing off the hook. News agencies are calling with questions about a situation of which you're completely unaware. Reporters are being aggressive with their questions and want answers because they have short deadlines. You don't have one ounce of situational awareness about what is happening with your organization.

Here is where crisis media relations differs from day-to-day media relations: It's all about a change in focus. As you create **crisis media relations collateral** (news releases, talking points, FAQs, media statements), new concepts become top of mind — uncertainty, urgency, accuracy, empathy, resolution and even possibly restitution. The media relations professional must employ all their sharpened media relations skills during the crisis, but instead of being macro focused on the overall media relations effort, they must become micro focused on the crisis situation at hand. All routine work will take a backseat until this issue is resolved.

Taking the First Steps

First things first: Take a deep breath and stay calm. You'll need to think clearly and professionally. Your organization is counting on you to provide quality public relations counsel to guide them through the crisis. They are counting on you to create crisis media relations collateral that explains what the organization is doing to resolve the crisis. They are also relying on you to either identify an appropriate spokesperson or take on that role yourself. Being overwhelmed is not an option during a crisis, and you must be able to manage your emotions. Remember to engage in self-care to get you through this situation. Some suggestions to help you get you through the crisis include:

- Take time to engage in diaphragmatic breathing — deep breathing exercises can calm your body and mind.
- Talk through the situation with a trusted peer or colleague (if appropriate).
- Drink plenty of water and eat healthy — this is not the time to eat a dozen donuts.
- Get some sleep when you can; you'll be glad you did when you can't.
- Concentrate on the positive — identify at least one victory each day to keep you and your team from feeling defeated.

The second step is to wait — wait to answer reporters' questions until you are ready. You need to employ your best *critical listening* skills to find out what reporters are asking and why. Capture contact information for each reporter who

From left: Joe Herron and Suzanne Horsley spoke with NBC news anchor Brian Williams for a "Dateline" special episode on the aftermath of the tornadoes that struck Tuscaloosa, Alabama, on April 27, 2011. The media training they had completed with the American Red Cross allowed them to quickly respond to national and international media requests during this chaotic and uncertain time. **Photo credit: Danelle Schlegelmilch/ American Red Cross.**

calls — name, phone number, email address, mobile number for texts, name of the news agency, date and time of the conversation, and their deadline. Log this information into a database as it will be useful when you update your media roster or evaluate media coverage. If multiple members of your team are taking media calls, make this database available to all so that they will know if the same reporter has contacted other team members.

When reporters call, listen carefully to their questions and ask follow-up questions to help clarify what they are looking for, what angle they may be taking and who else they may be talking to. You want to know as much as possible about what they want before you either answer their questions yourself or arrange an interview with a spokesperson or SME.

Once you have a better idea of the crisis at hand, start gathering accurate internal information and determine the severity of the situation. You'll want to approach your information gathering by anticipating what else you think reporters might ask — what follow-up questions might they have once you give them these initial details? As you are collecting your information, some members of your organization may be hesitant to share details with you. Reassure them that your responsibility is to protect the organization's reputation and that you need accurate information to create the talking points, FAQs, media statements and news releases. You also need to prepare the organization's spokesperson for all questions that could be posed to them by reporters during upcoming interviews.

Once you have all the details you can get (which may or may not be everything you need, but enough to start), create the crisis media relations collateral. You

<table>
<tr><td>

**Insights From a
Media Relations Pro**

</td><td>

To successfully conduct media relations during crisis, a media relations professional needs to understand what news agencies are looking for and trying to accomplish. Former CNN anchor Jonathan Aiken shares his insights gained from years of experience in a national media organization.

</td></tr>
</table>

Anticipate What the Media Want To Know Before They Know It

At the other end of the text, call or email you just received, a reporter is in a hurry and looking for basic information from you: immediate facts, usable quotes and a time line for further updates. Whatever the crisis at hand, it's the beginning of a relationship that will rapidly develop in a variety of ways, all of which will influence the success of your mission.

Media outlets play two roles during a crisis, sometimes simultaneously: (1) They are the outlets through which your information gets out; (2) they are also the inlet for negative stories about your organization or product, acting as a megaphone for allegations, information or misinformation that contradicts the case you're trying to make.

Early in the coverage of a crisis, media can often bypass broader issues in their quest for fresh details, so at this stage, it's important to stay focused on the *smaller* picture you're facing — gathering those immediate facts quickly and conveying them accurately. Speed and transparency at the front end of an event can reap dividends for you as the story develops and the attention refocuses less on the "what" and more on the "how and why," areas where your organization might face reputational risk, or worse.

Unless you're dealing with something immediately life-threatening or catastrophic, you'll find there will be time to build out your immediate crisis plan to deal with further developments. Broader issues may also emerge as a theme of media coverage as the story matures. Resist the urge to start dealing with them preemptively; there may not be enough facts or information on hand yet to anchor the direction you may want to take, so don't complicate things before you have a clearer picture of what you are facing.

Go back to the "5Ws." That's your playing field for now, because in addition to being a media relations specialist, you're also now a journalist of sorts, working for your client. The best way to play that role for your benefit (and theirs) is to use the media's role as an "outlet" to your best advantage. Do this by turning to your sources — the SMEs, well-briefed spokespersons or third-party verifiers — to post videos and/or still photos for sharing or downloading, FAQs, fact sheets and other materials that can offer a controlled conduit for your messaging.

Above all, be mindful of the space you're in. The early stages of crisis media coverage are often filled with speculation and assumption. Facts are rarely readily available, while hastily drawn conclusions often are, so it's best to avoid questions and side issues designed to take you there. There will be issues enough to deal with, without you contributing to your own workload.

Nature abhors a vacuum. So do news outlets, which is why it's critical to fill the "early space" of an event with facts and supporting details. It's not about controlling the story — you'll never be able to completely do that. Applying a football metaphor here, this is more about "time of possession"; the longer you can get an outlet to work with your information, the more it will tell your version of the story. That's important for more than just the obvious reason; it's also often the rough amount of time you'll have to catch your breath and start working on next steps, which will certainly involve developing answers for the next round of questions reporters will ask.

will need talking points and FAQs (see Chapter 8). These two documents are the foundation for your response to the who, what, when, where, why and how of the current crisis. These documents contain all the pertinent information that your spokespersons will need to successfully answer reporters' questions. In the event you and your team decide to decline an interview, you need to craft a media statement and use it as your response mechanism to the crisis.

Note: Before you finalize any version of your crisis media relations collateral, make sure you have had it reviewed by the organization's leadership. Then make sure each member of the organization's leadership team has a final copy to ensure consistency of messaging. The policies and procedures for approving messages during a crisis should already be part of your approved media relations plan.

Operating in a Crisis Command Center

During a crisis, a central control and command area may be established to ensure your organization's continuity of operations and response. The most important part of the **crisis command center** is the people who staff the center. Thus, key decision makers gather in one location — a large conference room, a separate facility or some other predesignated site — to respond to the crisis. The simple fact that you are responsible for protecting your organization's brand and creating the messaging makes you a key decision maker who must be included in this center.

Responding to a crisis in this fashion can prove to be very helpful. With all the decision makers in one place, it's easier for you to gather accurate and timely information regarding the crisis. It's also easier to seek clarity about what happened and how things are being resolved. This is so important when trying to ensure consistency in your messaging. It's also very convenient when needing to secure suggestions and approval for the messaging you are crafting.

There are some downsides to conducting crisis communication in a crisis command center: It can be noisy and filled with lots of commotion, making it hard to concentrate, and working in close proximity with your teammates may be challenging when you are tired and your emotions are running high. But the convenience of having important information and decision-making at your fingertips outweighs the challenges of a crisis command center.

Working in a Joint Information Center

Not all crises are confined to a single organization or geographic location. The crisis can manifest in a large weather event, earthquake or wildfire that affects multiple communities, or in the collapse of a single building that houses multiple businesses. In these situations, you may find yourself as part of a Joint Information System (JIS), which is the method of operating that allows multiple sources to coordinate efficiently and consistently, and you may be assigned to a **joint information center** (JIC)[1] — which is the central location that supports the operation.

Dianna Van Horn has worked in multiple JICs during her years with the American Red Cross and shared her expertise on how communicators can be successful in this environment. JICs may be formed at virtually any level: city, county, state or federal, such as one led by the Federal Emergency Management Agency (FEMA), but at each level you're almost certain to find representatives of law enforcement, emergency management, government, local businesses and community organizations. You should expect to be one among many individuals, each sharing the same goal: getting accurate information out to those who need it because during an emergency, getting the right information to the right people at the right time helps them to make the right decision.

Because the JIC is made up of public information officers (PIOs) from multiple organizations, it's critical that everyone be prepared to work together and understand the importance of message coordination even when PIOs may have competing priorities. Organizations participating in the JIC retain their autonomy, but the lead PIO must provide message guidance to avoid confusing the affected audience. Even before a JIC is established, public information functions must still be coordinated and integrated across jurisdictions and agencies, so it's always a good idea to identify and network with other PIOs in your area *now* to build relationships for the long term. Doing so will pay dividends not only during a disaster response but also during a crisis response within your organization.

As you work in a JIC, your focus will be objective-driven communication, always looking at three key points:

1. **Objective:** What are the incident needs? Why are you communicating?
2. **Audience:** Who are you trying to reach and what do they already know?
3. **Message:** What will you say and how will you say it? Which medium will work best?

Working in a JIC is important work that requires media relations professionals to be skilled in their field, flexible, detail oriented, professional and collegial. Doing so helps ensure that information is coordinated, misinformation is reduced and resources are maximized.

Practice Makes Perfect — Incorporating Crisis Into Your Training Program

As any athlete knows, it takes practice to improve one's skills. The same applies to being a spokesperson, especially during a crisis. You need trained spokespersons who can deliver the organizations' messaging accurately, show authority, convey knowledge, exude empathy and display a calm demeanor. There are many business professionals who believe that all it takes to be a spokesperson is the ability to stand in front of a microphone and answer a few questions from a reporter. *They are so wrong.* For this reason, as your organization's media relations professional, you should schedule spokesperson crisis training at least once a year.

Once you've identified a cadre of teammates to serve as spokespersons, it's time to set up a training that will help them create and deliver your organization's messaging. You'll want this training to simulate a potential crisis that could actually occur with your organization. The goal is for your designated spokespersons to practice and discuss their roles related to crises in a nonthreatening environment.

Insights From a Media Relations Pro

Scott McBride has worked in many joint information centers for disaster responses during his career in the U.S. Coast Guard. McBride shares his experience working in a JIC during the Deepwater Horizon Oil Spill and tells how he was suddenly taken off guard during a normally routine interaction with residents of the Gulf Coast community.

When Your Face Tells the Wrong Story

In July 2010 I was deployed to Mobile, Alabama, as a public information officer (PIO) in support of the Coast Guard's response to the Deepwater Horizon oil spill. The unified command decided to host a community engagement event in Pensacola, Florida, to provide updates on the federal response to the oil spill. The event, which was open to the public and the press, was hosted in a local hotel ballroom, where members of the unified command provided updates on response efforts.

At this point in the response, oil had washed up on the shores of Pensacola's pristine white beaches, which understandably created angst among local residents and negatively impacted tourism in the area. The community wanted to know when their beaches would be clean again.

In my role as PIO, I helped facilitate media interviews following the unified command update. During a break between interviews, while I was chatting with members of the public, a microphone appeared from beneath my arm; the microphone's source was a gentleman standing behind me. In my moment of bewilderment, another gentleman, who claimed to be a reporter, confronted me and asked if I had any children.

Just like that, I was in the middle of a media interview that I had not planned for. Not knowing where he was going with his question, I promptly replied that I had two sons. He quickly followed up his question asking me if I would let my children play on Pensacola's beaches. I hesitated to answer his question, and clearly showed my annoyance with him by my awkward facial reaction.

In that moment, I thought to myself, "What sort of question is that?" Yet my facial reaction told a different story, which the reporter capitalized on. To the reporter, my facial expression said, "Heck no, I would not let my kids on this beach." The reporter promptly picked up on that cue and said, "See ... even a Coast Guard officer won't let his kids on the beach, yet they are telling the public that the beaches are clean and safe."

In that moment, I learned a harsh lesson about the importance of nonverbal communication. Ninety-three percent of communication is nonverbal, therefore, you should be mindful of what your body language might be communicating. If you're not careful, your nonverbal communication may ultimately undermine or hinder the message you are trying to get across.

In my case, my nonverbal communication undermined my credibility as a spokesperson. Fortunately for me, the person posing as a reporter was not with a media organization, so my clip never gained any traction. But this experience will make me more mindful to avoid having this kind of reaction in the future.

One of your first objectives will be to identify and discuss how poor communication can hurt your organization. You'll want to explain the importance of successfully conducting media relations and the impact negative media coverage has on an organization — loss of productivity; loss of revenue; and loss of credibility with customers, stakeholders and the general public. One approach is to find a crisis that's been highlighted in the media and discuss what worked or didn't work and the consequences for the organizations involved.

In crisis media training, share your organization's overall key messages, which describe your organization and what it does. This will be a foundational resource of information as you begin to create talking points and FAQs for your crisis response (see Chapter 8 to help you develop key messages and talking points).

Written talking points establish consistent communication regarding a situation that your entire organization can use to answer questions from anyone. Talking points are a tool your spokesperson uses to convey your organization's messaging during the media interview, but they also can be used by a receptionist answering calls or your social media manager developing online content. Talking points need to be brief statements with the most important information your organization is trying to convey regarding the crisis at that moment in time.

There are some basic standard procedures to prepare for all interviews:

- Do a little research on the reporter and the news agency. You want to understand what their reporting style and potential angle may be.

- Have your messaging prepared and ready to use.

- For television, look professional and check your background. You want your target audience to listen and understand what you say and not be distracted by your appearance.

- For a radio interview, if you're in the studio, stay focused. If doing a phone interview, use a quiet office and use a landline if possible.

- For online interviews, find a quiet location and double-check to ensure your equipment and Wi-Fi signal are operating properly.

We will dive deeper into media interview preparation in Chapter 9. The bottom line is to be prepared for all types of questions. If you don't have key messages and talking points committed to memory, have them written down and easily accessible. Use your prepared messaging to respond to questions. Remember, your talking points are your lifeline. Avoid using jargon and acronyms. Use the key messages to close out your interview.

ACTION STEPS

Crisis media relations is not the same as routine media relations, and you and your team members must be prepared for the unexpected. While many of the skills and abilities are the same, in a crisis your approach to the situation, the manner in which you manage media inquiries and the way you deliver the information will be faster, more stressful and full of uncertainty for you and your key publics.

Complete the Action Steps for this chapter. Consider how your organization or client will respond in a crisis situation and develop media training components that will address these nonroutine events.

CHAPTER SEVEN ACTION STEPS: CRISIS PLANNING

Part A

Identify the policies and procedures your client or organization has in place for managing media inquiries. It is imperative to have these in place *before* a crisis hits.

1. Does your client or organization currently have a system for tracking media inquiries? If so, describe it. If not, this is a good time to draft a policy for accurately capturing the details we discussed at the beginning of this chapter. Using a database or spreadsheet makes it easier to track a story from inquiry to publication, analyze the reporters and media outlets that are most interested in your mission and share the information with all on the media relations team.

2. What is your policy for media calls? For example, do calls come to a central media number, where they are triaged, logged into the tracking system and then sent to members of the team for responses? Do individual members of your media relations team alternate taking calls? Is someone designated to take calls after business hours?

Part B

Identify the personnel and resources that are available from your organization during crises.

1. What types of crisis media relations collateral do you already have in place for responding to a crisis? What other pieces of communication might you need for your organization or client?

2. Who is the primary spokesperson for your client or organization? In the past year, has someone else served as spokesperson during a crisis situation? If so, who was that and what were the circumstances?

3. Does your client or organization have a plan for a crisis command center? If so, describe the plan or provide a link for easy access. If not, this is a good opportunity to earn leadership's support to develop one.

4. Has anyone from your organization had training or experience in a joint information center? If not, is there a partner or resource you can go to for training?

NOTE

[1] For more information on joint information centers, see FEMA's *National Incident Management System Basic Guidance for Public Information Officers*, available at https://www.fema.gov/sites/default/files/documents/fema_nims-basic-guidance-public-information-officers_12-2020.pdf.

Writing Key Messages and Talking Points

AGENDA

1. Learn the importance of key messages and talking points.
2. Determine the communication goal before writing your messages.
3. Understand how the messages are developed for media training.
4. Complete the Action Steps at the end of the chapter.

KEY CONCEPTS

Key Messages
Talking Points
Communication Goals

Written Preparation Grounds Training in Reality

Just as you would for a real media interview, you must have written materials prepared in advance for training. Media relations training would be pointless if the participants were simply making up facts as they went along. Whether you are conducting training for a college class or a Fortune 500 company, you want to provide a meaningful learning experience that will empower the participants to engage in the next media opportunity.

Learning to write organizational messaging is a valuable skill that will pay off in all of your media relations efforts. Depending upon the role your participants have in the organization, you may wish to include them in the writing exercises. For example, if you are training the CEO or subject matter experts for an upcoming interview, you would have the written materials already prepared for them. However, if you are training individuals to work on an active media relations team, it would be valuable to include a writing exercise in your training program.

Developing and writing each of these materials will not only enhance your own understanding of the organization but will ensure that everyone on your media relations team is speaking with one voice on all issues. When time is of the essence, your spokesperson will thank you as you hand them the most recent update on a situation instead of guessing what the priorities should be during the interview.

Preparing the Documents

The two primary written materials that this chapter covers are key messages and talking points. **Key messages** are the standard facts about your organization (or issue) that are relatively static, meaning they don't change often. These facts may include the mission statement, employment statistics, the corporate social responsibility (CSR) program or details on the product or service offerings. Also, during a crisis, such as a layoff or employee malfeasance, you may not be able to discuss

When working with partner organizations on issues or events, it is imperative to share information for seamless continuity of messaging. During an April 2013 special event to honor wounded military personnel, the American Red Cross and the U.S. Moral, Welfare and Recreation Office in Garmisch-Partenkirchen, Bavaria, Germany, teamed up to conduct a series of media interviews to promote the cause. Media relations representatives from each organization worked together to develop the key messages and talking points for the event. **PHOTO CREDIT: PETER MACÍAS.**

certain details. However, drafting key messages can help you articulate what is *typically* done in these situations while outlining related policies and procedures.

There is no limit on the types of information you may include in key messages, so you may need targeted documents that address overall topics. For example, you may have an entire key message document about product lines and another about the CSR program. Generally, the spokesperson should commit these facts to memory for easy recall during the media interview.

Much of the content for key messages will be readily available on the organization's website, in the last annual report or in a company brochure. It's a matter of gathering, summarizing, and organizing the details so a member of the media relations team can review them for a quick refresher. None of these facts should be new to the spokesperson who should already be an expert on your organization, which is why you have invited them to join the team. Since this information is not proprietary or likely to change soon, you are welcome to share the document with a reporter.

For the American Red Cross, for example, the key messages may include the organization's mission to help during disasters, the list of organizing principles, basic facts about the location of the Red Cross chapter office and explanations of how the Red Cross typically responds to specific disasters.

Talking points are much more specific and time sensitive than key messages. Because the information changes so quickly, you may need to refer to the latest draft during your interview, press conference or public meeting. Talking points are essential for a variety of nonroutine events, such as a crisis, changes in leadership, an upcoming large-scale special event or a product launch.

The fluid nature of talking points requires that they have a date and time stamp to identify the most recent version, and they should never be handed over to reporters who may end up using old information in a story. Gathering information for talking points can be a challenging task, and you may wish to designate a team member who will do continuous fact checks and updates. Your media relations plan should have procedures in place for verification and approval of all publicly shared information, so be sure the appointed team member follows the established policies before sharing any updated documents.

Prioritizing the talking points will help your spokesperson organize their thoughts during the interview. Bullet points of three essential messages for that point in time will allow the spokesperson to circle back to those items while answering the media's questions. At the conclusion of the interview, when the reporter inevitably asks if there is anything the spokesperson wishes to add, they can summarize those priority messages to ensure the public receives that information.

Returning to the Red Cross example, talking points may include details about how many volunteers are helping at a disaster response, how many meals were served to disaster victims and first responders, how many homes were affected by the disaster and how many families slept at the disaster shelter last night.

Figure 8.1 offers a summary of how these documents are formatted and shared. Organizations maintain these documents on file, update them regularly and integrate them into their training sessions so that all members of the media relations team are familiar with the material.

Key Messages	
Definition:	Are evergreen and should be drafted and committed to memory well in advance of an interview.
Purpose:	Are used for general facts and explanations about the organization, such as mission, values, position on issues, details about product or service lines, employment stats, general fundraising or financial facts, and other activities that typically don't change often.
Format:	The document is titled "Key Messages," printed on organization letterhead, has date of last revision, and has internal contact information for questions or additional information.
Availability:	The "Key Messages" document should be shared with key players within the organization. The details in this document are typically available on websites and in materials shared with media and stakeholders.
Talking Points	
Definition:	Details about specific, nonroutine events that can change by the hour, day or week; the points address the current situation and priorities.
Purpose:	Typically used for a crisis, special event, fundraising campaign, changes in leadership or any other rapidly evolving activity.
Format:	The document is titled "Talking Points," marked for "Internal Use Only," printed on organization letterhead, has date and time of last revision, and has contact information for the person responsible for updates.
Availability:	"Talking Points" documents change rapidly and should not be shared with the public or media. TPs are used by leaders, SMEs and spokespersons during information exchanges such as interviews, news conferences, or public meetings.

Figure 8.1   Messaging for media interviews.

Articulating Your Communication Goals

Your talking points will relate to a communication goal that you have in that particular moment. **Communication goals** can:

1. Create *awareness* for your target publics about the current topic.
2. Change the *attitude* of your target publics about the current topic.
3. Encourage an *action* or behavioral change concerning the current topic.

Consider this scenario:

You are the media relations manager for a large United Way agency in the Midwest, and you are developing talking points for the launch of your annual giving campaign. The development director is planning an outdoor event to thank last year's top corporate donors and to announce the fundraising goal for this year. For a small donation, people can attend the special launch party featuring food and drinks donated by area restaurants, free giveaways from local retailers and live music by a popular band. A reporter from the local news has called to ask for an interview about the upcoming campaign. This reporter usually covers financial news along with some government and nonprofit stories.

As you draft your talking points, what are your communication goals? What are the most important facts you want to share with the reporter? What are the three things you want the newspaper's readers to remember about the campaign launch?

Having a mix of communication goals can provide the most benefit from a media appearance.

1. Awareness is the easiest goal to accomplish — the basic *who, what, when,* and *where* answers will inform the audience about the upcoming event.

2. Changing attitudes is more difficult — the public needs to be convinced as to *how* this campaign is going to help the community and that the United Way is actually serving the public good.

3. Creating action is the most difficult — being aware of the event and having a positive attitude about United Way is not enough to get people to attend and donate. The *why* question becomes the most important here: Why is it important for me to physically go to this campaign launch and support them with my money?

For this scenario with this reporter, your top three talking points might include these facts:

1. Date, time, location and cost of admission. (Awareness)

2. Emphasize that all the food, prizes and entertainment are being donated, demonstrating that the United Way is being a good steward of donations by putting the admission fees into community programs. (Attitude)

3. Highlight a United Way program that has made a significant difference in the community. Programs like that can't happen without financial donations from all members of the community. Attending the launch party will be a fun and easy way to support these programs. (Action)

Practicing the Messages

For your media training program, it's easy to put messaging into practice and get your SMEs, leadership team and media relations staff comfortable with the material. You or your team can generate a set of key messages for your organization along with prioritized talking points for a typical event or activity at your place of business. If you have a significant event coming up, use those event talking points for this exercise. This exercise should be realistic, not hypothetical.

Pair up the training participants and ask them to take turns being the reporter and the spokesperson. The role play will accomplish several goals: help the participants learn to think like a reporter and anticipate their questions, test their recall ability of the key messages and talking points and allow them to practice thinking on their feet in a fast-paced communication setting. The partners then give each other feedback, noting accuracy of facts, ability to stay on message and flexibility to respond to the reporter's questions while returning to the priority talking points.

This low-stress exercise can be a warm-up for a larger simulation activity or a simple refresher. In the chapter exercise, you will develop your own key messages and talking points that will be used in your future media training exercises.

<table>
<tr><td>

Insights From a Media Relations Pro

</td><td>

Crisis management was a common task while Greg Trevor was managing public information for the Port Authority of New York, and he thought he was prepared — most of the time. During this particular instance, Trevor realized too late that his talking points were not as complete as he thought. He shares this case to highlight the importance of anticipating all the questions before you go on camera, or in this case, go live on radio.

</td></tr>
</table>

There's No Room for Improvisation in Media Relations

In March 2001 I was working as an information officer for The Port Authority of New York and New Jersey — which manages, among other areas, the bridges connecting the two states as well as the area's airports and seaports.

When weather forecasters predicted that a major snowstorm would hit the area, we transitioned to 12-hour shifts around the clock. A few hours before the storm hit, I was doing a live radio interview with WCBS-AM in New York, one of the region's most listened to 24-hour news outlets.

After I provided a rundown of flight cancellations and bridge-speed restrictions, the radio host said, "You know Greg, I've always wanted to ask this question: Who decides when to close the seaports?" He was referring to the ports that manage the major container ships that provide goods to 18 million people across the region.

Unfortunately, I was not prepared to answer this question, so I did the worst thing a spokesperson can do — I started to improvise, rattling off a list that included our agency, the shipping lines, the Coast Guard and about a half-dozen other groups.

I got off the air quickly, hoping that no one had heard my major mistake. About three minutes later I got a call from a laughing Scott Weinberger, who at the time was an investigative reporter with WNBC-TV.

"Hey Greg, I was driving home, and I heard you on the radio. You forgot Popeye the Sailor Man!" Much to my embarrassment, one of the leading reporters in the New York media market had heard my random list of agencies that may or may not be involved in making these decisions.

The incident occurred because our office was so fixated at the time on answering questions about storm management at the airports, we did not discuss the ports in advance of the media inquiries. We learned two lessons:

1. When you prepare for media inquiries, try to anticipate any question you might be asked — not just the questions that are most likely.
2. There's no shame in admitting you cannot answer a question — even during a live interview.

ACTION STEPS

Prepare for your team's training exercises by generating key messages and talking points for your organization. You will use the chart in Figure 8.1 to construct your documents, and you may need to refer back to the chapter material to complete your assignment. Once you have drafted your documents, you and your team will practice using your key messages and talking points in interviews. The documents you create here will be used again in later Action Steps.

Complete the Action Steps for this chapter, using real facts from your organization, class client or another organization of your choice: Draft talking points and key messages; pair up with a partner to role-play the spokesperson and the reporter in a simulated interview; and evaluate your efforts to recall key messages and talking points accurately.

CHAPTER EIGHT ACTION STEPS:
DEVELOPING KEY MESSAGES AND TALKING POINTS

Part A

For this Action Step, you will use real facts from your own organization, class client or another organization of your choice. Regardless of what organization you use, the facts should not be manipulated because accuracy of statements is one of the ways you will evaluate your team members. Use the formatting tips provided in Figure 8.1.

1. **Key Messages:** Draft key messages for your organization. As mentioned in the chapter, you may need to focus on a particular topic or function of your organization to create a single, concise document. For example, your key messages may focus on the organization's history, on the product or service line or on a charitable initiative.

2. **Talking Points:** Draft prioritized (ranked) talking points about a nonroutine event that has either happened in the past or is coming up for your organization. Make the talking points as factual as possible and put the most important ones at the top of the list. Be sure to have a mix of communication goals: awareness, attitude and action. Are the top three talking points the ones you really want your target publics to remember? Is there an action goal among the top three?

Once you have drafted your documents, you and your team will practice using your key messages and talking points in interviews.

Part B

Have your team members practice using your key messages and talking points. Draft a brief scenario about the reporter's inquiry, and then pair up your group members to take turns being the reporter and the spokesperson. Allow about 10 minutes for each role play. At the conclusion, ask partners to give each other feedback noting accuracy of facts, ability to stay on message and flexibility to respond to the reporter's questions while returning to the priority talking points.

1. Provide a brief evaluation of the reporter and their inquiry. _____

2. Rate each spokesperson on their use of key messages and talking points using this simple scorecard. This can be used by the trainers as well as by other participants as part of peer evaluation.

Accuracy of facts:	1 2 3 4 5
	Comments:
Successful inclusion of top talking points:	1 2 3 4 5
	Comments:
Ability to respond to reporter's questions while staying on message:	1 2 3 4 5
	Comments:
Successful concluding state-ment with at least one talking point with an action goal:	1 2 3 4 5
	Comments:

chapter **9**

Preparing for Interviews
in All Formats

AGENDA

1. Learn how to prepare physically and mentally for the interview.
2. Practice video conferencing skills to be your own camera operator.
3. Know when to speak and when to shut up.
4. Learn strategies for dealing with difficult reporters.
5. Complete the Action Steps at the end of the chapter.

KEY CONCEPTS

Single Overriding Communication Objective (SOCO)
Interruptible Feedback (IFB)
Soundbite
Bridging and Flagging

The Three P's of Interviews:
Prepare, Practice, Perform

If you haven't caught on to the theme that's been threaded through the last few chapters, it's prepare and practice, prepare and practice, and prepare and practice. Most communication professionals are hip deep in trying to feed *the beast* that is the 24-hour-a-day news cycle. The media relations pro is researching data, images and sound and working diligently to create the most compelling stories possible to highlight the amazing work being conducted by your organization. So, who has time to draft FAQs and talking points or conduct mock interviews for a situation that might or might not happen? You do!

With the proliferation of digital news outlets, the explosion of viral news via social media, a lack of trust in institutions, bloggers as influencers, citizen journalists and "gotcha" journalism, it's more important than ever to be able to "*control and deliver*" your message. Therefore, you need to prepare, practice and perform. This chapter describes how you and your media relations team will *prepare* for interviews in all forms and *practice* for them in controlled exercises. However, it is up to the media relations manager to ensure the training pays off with opportunities for all the team members to *perform* in an actual media interview. It's a much different situation once it's for real and not in an exercise environment.

No matter how many times a spokesperson has been interviewed by the news media, it's prudent to conduct some prep work. The goal is to deliver the organization's message with confidence, authority and knowledge. Does the spokesperson have a grasp of the talking points? Are they "camera ready?" Are they comfortable with the medium in which they are being interviewed? Delivering a quality media interview is as important as the actual message itself.

Why the Medium Matters

In this chapter, we will go into great detail about how you and your media relations team will prepare, practice and perform in all different types of interviews. The medium will make a great deal of difference in how you deliver your message, how detailed your responses are, what collateral material you offer to the journalist and even who you choose to do the interview. While your key messages and talking points will be the same, the way you prepare, respond to questions, and frame your answers will vary based upon the media format.

Figure 9.1 summarizes the various types of media formats and what to expect from each one. Figure 9.2 gives suggestions from media trainers for how to practice before that particular interview. Next, we go into detail about how you can help your team and spokespersons prepare and practice for each media format.

Television Interviews

We all recognize that television is a visual medium, but have you considered what visuals you bring to an on-camera interview? The audience consuming this type of media is looking to see what is happening, know where it's happening and understand to whom it's happening. Research has found that an adult in the United States spends an average of 8 hours and 47 minutes per day watching screens — smartphones, tablets, computers, gaming consoles or television. Ninety percent of information transmitted to the human brain is visual, and the visuals are processed by the brain 60,000 times faster than text.[1] For this very reason, it is imperative that you are well prepared for an interview in front of a camera.

Understanding Differences in Media Platforms		
TYPE OF MEDIA		
PRINT	BROADCAST	ONLINE
Attributes of the story — More in-depth / Needs visuals / Longer deadlines / More interviewees	More sound bites / Video/B-roll/sound / Faster deadlines / Fewer interviewees	Depth varies / All visuals/audio + Links / Deadlines vary / Interviewees vary
Distribution of the story — Newspapers, magazines, online	Radio, TV, and online	Linked everywhere
Format of the interview — In-person, over the phone, email, and video conference interviews	Live, recorded, IFB, video conference, call-in, news desk interviews	All types of interviews, especially video conference

FIGURE 9.1   Working with different media.

A wise man once said, "If not for the visuals of television, it would just be radio." Conducting a television interview has evolved so much over the years. At one time you just walked into a television studio or met a reporter at a designated site and conducted an interview. Today a television interview can be conducted from anywhere in the world, as long as the reporter or you have a capable smartphone, tablet or laptop and a quality cell or Wi-Fi signal. But there are still some basics that are important to know.

There are several points that you or your designated spokesperson must remember when preparing for the television interview. First, and most important, do you have the most accurate and up-to-date key messages and talking points with which to conduct the interview (this goes for all interviews, no matter what the media format)? Be ready with your **Single Overriding Communication Objective (SOCO)**, the most important information you want your audience to know. If the target audience hears nothing else, they must hear and understand

Rehearsal Tips for Each Interview Type	
Radio	Practice with a colleague over the phone.
TV	Practice using a camera or mirror.
IFB	Answer questions using earbuds in a noisy room.
Print/Web	Create simpler explanations of complicated issues that resonate with the audience. Practice storytelling.
Video Calls	Rehearse with a colleague using the same equipment and video conferencing software that you will use for interview.
ALL Types	Own those key messages and talking points! Predict the tough questions. Practice empathy & being human — it's harder than you think.

FIGURE 9.2   How to practice for interviews.

your SOCO. Follow up the SOCO with key messages and talking points (see Chapter 8) that contain facts: research and statistics that provide solid support for the statement(s) or idea(s) that you've made. But remember, information is just information unless you humanize it and make it relevant. Paint a word picture that weaves color and real examples that support your SOCO.

Many professional communicators memorize their key messages and talking points for interviews. But even the most seasoned communicator can get a little nervous and lose track of their messaging. As a backup, handwrite your messaging on a steno pad and have it in your hand during the interview. You may not need to refer to your notes, but you should have them in case you need them.

Second, since television is such a visual communication medium and your goal is for your audience to consume and remember your message, it's important

During this live interview for the "Today Show," Lester Holt, NBC News anchor, and Oscar Barnes, American Red Cross chapter director (left to right, center of photo), update viewers on the response efforts following the April 27, 2011, tornado in Tuscaloosa, Alabama. The number of news staff and the amount of equipment used for interviews on location varies by the type of media outlet. National broadcast operations such as NBC News sent multiple reporters, producers, camera operators and sound technicians to conduct in-depth reporting at multiple sites, creating several opportunities for spokespersons to share the disaster recovery story. Smaller local news organizations, however, often sent a single reporter to the site, resulting in fewer opportunities for spokespersons to gain coverage in those media markets. Photo credit: J. Suzanne Horsley.

to minimize visual distractions. For example, if your interview is at your place of business, you can choose a background for your interview that will tell the viewer where you are but will not be too distracting. You don't want a noisy environment or people moving around in the shot. Your background may be a company sign, the front of a building, or a step-and-repeat backdrop of your logo. Depending on your topic, you may want to showcase work or activities happening in the distant background, featured products or relevant equipment. Be creative about your background, but don't overdo it.

Third, besides your background, you should be aware of your nonverbals during an interview. The overuse of hand gestures, tossing your hair, fixing your tie, adjusting your eyeglasses or fidgeting with jewelry can divert the audience's attention away from what you're trying to say. Stop waving those hands around! Practice finding a way to ground yourself during an interview so that you use hand gestures only when they can help you make a point, not detract from it.

Fourth (this may seem a little vain), but make sure you have the right attire and appearance for the interview. Ask yourself a few questions:

- Am I dressed properly to represent my organization? This may range from having actual logos on your clothes to wearing clothes that represent the work you do.
- Does my attire allow the organization's logo to be seen clearly in the background?
- Am I properly groomed — is my hair combed, is my face not too shiny and is there nothing in my teeth?
- Do my eyeglasses create too much glare from the lighting? Feel free to ask the camera operator.

Remember that, in general, the reporter and camera operator want you to look good. Before the interview begins, feel free to ask the videographer if your organization's branding is clearly visible or if your eyeglasses are creating a glare from the lights. It's acceptable to ask the videographer to see the composition of the shot before you start the interview. They know that if there is something embarrassing in the shot, your fly is open or there are distractions in the background, this will make *their* work look unprofessional. They want you to succeed in the interview so that they have a good product to air on television.

If possible, record your interview when it airs or download it from the media agency's website. This affords you a copy of everything that was said in case there were any inaccuracies, and it provides data to add to your media audit and an opportunity to evaluate the interview. Don't ask the reporter for a copy; that's unprofessional and tells the reporter that you don't watch their program or know how to locate stories on their website or social channels. You want the reporter to ask you for another interview in the future, so don't waste their time.

Being Your Own Camera Operator for Remote or Online Interviews

Remote interviews via video conferencing platforms are now prevalent in the news media industry, so practicing in this setting is an essential part of your media training. The advantage is that you become the videographer and have complete control over the visual presentation of your interview. The disadvantage is that it's up to you to ensure your electronic equipment and cell or Wi-Fi signal are operating at optimum capacity. Many of us have experienced a sudden loss of a cell or Wi-Fi signal, or the battery dying on our electronic devices in the middle of a conversation. If this happens during an important media interview, it can be detrimental to the business goal you're trying to accomplish.

Now that your equipment is ready to go, check the background for the remote interview (see photos). You'll want to set up your equipment to ensure that you have a well-composed visual. Be sure you are the key element on the screen and the background looks professional and doesn't distract from the important information you're trying to share. Have visual cues in the frame that will show viewers who you are: a step-and-repeat backdrop with your logo, company signage or a logo on your shirt are simple ways to ensure the public knows who you are representing. Avoid using virtual backgrounds because they can create a fragmented or blurred image that will distract the viewer. The experiences you undoubtedly have had over Zoom or Skype will pay off when you are working to manage your visuals for an interview.

Lighting is an important aspect of your visual composition for the interview. Ensure that your light source is not at your back because it causes your face to be in complete darkness. Be aware of overly bright or direct lighting that can cause

When conducting remote interviews using videoconferencing platforms, give yourself a chance to be successful by thinking like a news camera operator. It is distracting for the viewer when the camera is pointing up someone's nose (as in the first photo) or when the lighting is too dark. Position your laptop or mobile device to ensure good eye contact with the reporter (as in the second photo). If needed, stack a few books or boxes under your device to properly position your camera so that the reporter, and thus the audience, can look you in the eye. Test the background view and lighting before the interview is scheduled to begin. Most importantly, remember to look at the camera lens instead of the reporter's face on your screen. PHOTO CREDIT: PETER MACÍAS.

shadows across your face. When possible, use a natural light source to enhance your image. You may want to invest in a ring light that lessens shadows and diffuses light evenly across the subject's face.

Don't forget your sound quality. The internal mic on a computer or smartphone may not be clear enough, especially if there are any environmental noises. External mics are inexpensive devices that will immensely improve the quality of your sound. You can use anything from a noise canceling headset to a less noticeable lavalier mic. Test your mic as part of your rehearsal.

Don't try setting up for an online interview at the last second. You need to be concentrating on your message delivery. Start ahead of time to choose the background for the interview and practice setting up your equipment. Determine the best lighting source that is available to you. Video conference with a colleague or friend and practice, practice, practice using the exact same equipment and internet connection that you will use during the interview.

Tips for On-Camera Media Training

The training experience for on-camera interviews should be as authentic as possible. For example, if the interview is recorded for editing and airing at a later time, the reporter may ask several questions that require in-depth answers. While it's unlikely that a reporter will air a long statement, they often do this to gather background information for them to summarize and synthesize into their news stories. You can tell when they are asking for background and when they are looking for a soundbite, but that takes practice. Incorporating all the ways reporters will work to construct their stories is an essential element of the training exercise.

In your training sessions, make the mock interviews as realistic as possible. Use real cameras and good lighting and record the interviews to play back later in critique sessions. Have the person playing the reporter (who should have media experience) ask the participant to state and spell their name and give their job title. The reporter should ask a mix of questions that require detailed responses (for background) and short, concise responses (for soundbites). A **soundbite**, on average, is 9 to 12 seconds, so have your training participants practice delivering their priority talking points, or SOCOs, with a stopwatch.

In addition to rehearsing with real camera equipment, be sure to practice using **interruptible feedback** (also referred to as interruptible foldback or interrupt for broadcast) **(IFB)** earpieces — earbuds can simulate this experience, too. IFBs are used for remote interviews when the interviewee is on location and the anchor or producer is conducting the interview from the studio. Typically, there is no reporter on scene, and the videographer will set up the interview and hand the interviewee an earpiece; then the newsperson in the studio takes over. These interviews can be uncomfortable because the interviewee is listening to crosstalk from the studio through their earpiece while staring into a fisheye lens on the camera. As we authors can attest, we were thankful that we rehearsed IFB interviews in a controlled exercise setting before we had to deliver one in the field.

Insights From a Media Relations Pro

Melissa Jackson draws from more than 25 years of experience in the broadcast industry to remind media trainers that it takes more than talking points filled with facts and figures to make your story resonate with the audience. Here she shares a lesson she learned while helping a subject matter expert prepare for an interview.

Getting Personal

When I first started one-on-one media training with scientists, researchers and educators at a large university, I met a variety of experts who were either excited, nervous or, in some cases, reluctant to improve their media skills. They walked into a professionally lit studio to meet me and a videographer intent on putting them through the paces. We picked apart their language, pacing and vocal tone, as well as if their eyes fluttered, their hands crept and their feet tapped. As a former television journalist, I thoroughly evaluated their verbal and nonverbal messaging.

Before the training sessions, I asked these media candidates to think through 3-5 primary points relating to their expertise. For those who practiced, it invariably led to a well-rehearsed elevator speech. While adequate for a short soundbite, it was exactly the opposite of what a television journalist desires for a profile or longer issue story. Broadcasters crave a conversational interview with an enthusiastic and authentic person.

I remember coaching a highly esteemed researcher who had developed a critical new approach in breast cancer detection. The subject matter was highly technical, and we worked hard to break down the scientific jargon into an understandable level of relevance.

What the researcher was not prepared for was a spontaneous set of more personal questions: "What are the thoughts that go through your own mind when you go through the mammogram process?" "What do you dream of for your own daughter in the future when it comes to breast cancer detection?" She answered initially with hesitation. It's a common response.

Some experts embrace questions that have a personal edge, and others will do anything to navigate around them. I've had a few researchers balk, feeling their research was demeaned or a reporter didn't understand the significance of their findings. Some might ask with subtle or not-so-subtle irritation, "What does my personal opinion have to do with my research?"

I acknowledge that their personal opinion does not always play a big role. At other times, it's the driving force.

"Did you always feel you would get into this field, or what launched this journey for you?" I asked. The breast cancer scientist paused, her face changing every few seconds like sunlight at the end of a day. She explained how she had planned to pursue another direction as a young woman until her own mother was diagnosed with breast cancer. I'd found the heart of her mission. For television, I would have unwrapped her remarkable scientific findings around this bittersweet nugget. She was surprised this detail was important to the story.

Part of a journalist's job is to break through the expected and find what causes an interview subject's eyes to spark on an emotional grid. Viewers remember passion, joy or sadness far longer than statistics and facts. Interviewees should set their own boundaries for a television interview, yet seriously consider getting personal. In a complex media world, the value is simple human connection.

The reporter should ask, "Is there anything else you'd like to add?" at the end of the mock interview. Train your participants to *always* take advantage of this opportunity to clearly articulate their SOCO. Typically, by the end of the interview, the interviewee has relaxed, settled into a rhythm and has already taken a few stabs at providing a soundbite, so they usually nail it at the close of the interview. More than likely, the statement they give at the end is the one that will end up in the broadcast.

Other things to practice for television:

- **Where to Look:** For interviews with a reporter, you should look at the reporter. If the interview is remote, look at the camera as if looking at the anchor person. If you aren't sure, ask the reporter or camera operator.

- **Avoid Unnecessary Words:** Don't use the reporter's name when answering questions because a different reporter may end up presenting the story later. Avoid saying "as I said before," "that's a good question," and "thanks for that question." Your statements will be edited for the final story, and you want to make it easy for the editor to choose good soundbites.

- **Where to Put Your Hands:** Hold something, like a notebook, to focus your nervous energy. Ask the videographer how much of your body will be in the camera view. Tell the reporter in advance if you have an important prop to show the audience.

Radio Interviews

When a radio reporter requests an interview, your preparation will be the same as what you do for television. The biggest difference between television and radio interviews is in how the interview is recorded. Unlike a television interview, in which you likely have a reporter and a videographer on scene, radio interviews are more likely to be conducted remotely.

Here are some ways to prepare for a radio interview:

- Check the equipment you are using in advance. This may include your cell phone, tablet, computer, earbuds or Wi-Fi signal. Be sure your equipment is fully charged and operating properly.

- Have your key messages and talking points at your fingertips for reference.

- Have a sip of water or a lozenge before the interview to clear you throat. You need to speak clearly.

- Find a quiet room for your interview, locking the door if necessary to avoid interruptions. Check to ensure there are no environmental noises (such as AC units or running equipment) that may create an audible distraction.

- Again, be confident in your messaging and the delivery of your message.

- If your interview is in the radio studio, all sound issues will be managed for you, and you will have the added benefit of speaking face-to-face with the reporter. Take advantage of this opportunity to develop relationships with the reporter and pitch additional stories.

Depending upon the format of the radio story, they may be looking for in-depth analysis or short soundbites. Confirm with the reporter before the interview if this is a live discussion, a question-and-answer format, or a prerecorded interview that will be edited during production. This will change the way you prepare: Longer analysis allows opportunities for storytelling, whereas shorter responses mean you need to practice paring down those messages into soundbites.

Just as with television, record the interview when it airs or find it online to add to your media coverage analysis and for you and others to view and provide feedback.

Tips for Radio Interview Training

Many of the tips we offered above for television interview training also apply to radio. Just remember that the *delivery* of the interview on radio is the key difference.

- **Use Your Phone:** Practice radio interviews with the trainer over the phone or while using earbuds. Because most radio interviews are done remotely, you will not have the advantage of being in front of the reporter and getting feedback from visual cues, such as smiles, head nods or confused expressions. Therefore, you should practice under the same circumstances.

- **Enunciate:** Focus on clearly articulating your words. If there are terms from your industry that turn into tongue twisters, practice saying them aloud. Avoid all organizational jargon. Speak a bit more slowly than you do in normal conversation.

- **Warm Up:** Do deep breathing exercises and practice your talking points by speaking into a large room (or outdoors). Try standing while talking on the phone to see how that opens up your diaphragm and helps you project your voice. You need a strong, clear voice for radio; nothing makes a listener change the station faster than a weak voice that's hard to understand.

- **Remind the Listeners Who You Are:** Because there are no visual cues for the radio, repeating your organization's name can help listeners remember who's talking or catch up if they tune in after the introductions. Don't be annoying about it, but every so often say, "We at XYZ Company are doing ... " or "One of XYZ's goals is ... " so that the listener knows who you are representing.

The Print Interview

As we have reminded you throughout this chapter, preparation is key — know your message, know your interviewer, be ready for all kinds of questions, breathe and deliver. Here are a few nuances about print interviews that you need to be aware of before you start:

- A print interview can be in-person or over the phone. Most of the time the interview is conducted by phone, and sometimes by email.

- Usually, this type of interview takes more time to complete than a television or radio interview. The reporter may spend more time asking background questions to help them understand the situation and to use in their analysis of the issue.

- The print reporter has more time to interview additional people and conduct their own analysis than most broadcast reporters. Therefore, some of their questions may have come from the other interviews they have already completed.

- The reporter can ask in-depth questions and is acutely aware of your physical, professional and emotional demeanor as you respond. For example, if you appear surprised or angered by a question, your reaction may make the reporter curious enough to ask more questions that reveal the reasons for your reaction.

- No matter if the reporter's publication is a printed newspaper or magazine, your words will end up both in print and online. The life of the resulting story can live on.

Once the story runs, save the story in its print and online versions and add these to your media coverage data collection and to your training materials for future use.

Training Tips for Print Interview Preparation

There are many overconfident people who think they can conduct a successful interview by just shooting from the hip. Don't get caught in that mindset. Mock interviews should prepare spokespersons to manage all aspects of the print interview:

- Help your trainees organize their thoughts and practice their messaging. Your goal is for them to be comfortable speaking as an SME and to speak with confidence.

- Demonstrate for your participants how to ask the reporter questions pre- and post-interview. For example: What's the subject of the interview? Are you interviewing anyone else on this subject? How will you use this information? When and where will the article be printed?

- Help your trainees understand what makes a suitable location for a face-to-face interview, preferably one that is quiet where they won't be disturbed. Reporters may already know where they want to do the interview, but remind your participants that they can negotiate the interview location if they foresee any problems with a proposed setting.

- Remind them to breathe and relax. They should treat the print interview as a conversation so that they don't appear nervous or fidgety.

- Have your exercise reporters take each trainee through a long-format print interview. Help the trainees practice storytelling techniques that will illustrate the talking points and SOCO.

- If the print interview is remote, tell your trainees they should use a landline phone and the handset. They should stand up, open the diaphragm, and speak clearly.
- Remind your training participants to be professional, polite and gracious with the reporter. It's not necessary, but a quick "thank you" note is a gesture that can separate them from others in their industry.
- Because they will probably spend more time with a print reporter than broadcast reporters, encourage your trainees to be wary of becoming too friendly during the interview. Anything they say or do while they are with the reporter can end up in the story.
- If your participants follow your training and advice, reporters will recognize their expertise and quality message delivery and will likely return to them for future interviews.

For All Formats: How to Prepare and When to Shut Up

Be a student of the news. Watch, listen and dissect how interviews are conducted; adapt styles you admire and make them your own. You will never know what to expect in different interview formats if you aren't studying all the formats yourself. While you are watching news stories, pay particular attention to whether the person being interviewed deliberately stops speaking once they've made their point or whether they seem to ramble on without a point in sight.

The key to successfully delivering your message during an interview is knowing what you want to say before you say it. Prepare your message with the top three things you need your audience to know and be prepared to provide supporting facts. You'll overwhelm the target audience if you try to squeeze in more than three talking points.

When delivering your three talking points, use simple declarative sentences. Read your messages aloud to hear how they sound and to practice their smooth delivery. Time yourself to see if you are within the time frame of a soundbite (9-12 seconds) or a more in-depth story (no more than 30 seconds at a time). If you need to take a breath while you're speaking, the sentences are too long. Do not use organizational jargon or acronyms; you'll lose the audience because they won't understand what you're talking about.

Once you've shared your messages and supported them with facts, stop talking. If you start rambling, you might say something the reporter will latch on to that will turn the interview in a direction you weren't anticipating. How does a reporter tempt you to elaborate beyond your prepared message? They often use one of these questioning techniques:

- Asking questions before you believe the interview has started. When talking to a reporter, you are always on the record!

- Asking rapid-fire questions to fluster you.
- Interrupting your answer with other questions.
- Using the phrase "really" or "you don't say" or "come on, now" to get you to say more than you should.
- Posing questions about another organization or asking you to respond to what another organization may or may not have said or done.
- Silence. Head nodding and complete silence from the reporter can be awkward. It's not your job to fill gaps in the conversation. Don't be tempted to fill the uncomfortable silence.

How to Deal With Aggressive Reporters and Keep Your Cool

The best method for dealing with an aggressive reporter is twofold: be prepared and keep your cool. Anticipate questions you are *most* likely to be asked; anticipate questions you are *least* likely to be asked; and anticipate questions you *don't want* to be asked. And be prepared to answer all these questions. Remember that your primary mission is to deliver your talking points.

Take control of the interview and focus on your talking points. Remember:

- Reporters can ask anything they like, and you can answer in any way you like.
- You *don't* have to answer questions, but you *do* have to deliver the message.
- Share good anecdotes to help make the story come alive.
- Have accurate statistics and examples at your fingertips to support what you're saying.

Being confronted by an aggressive reporter can be nerve-racking and challenging. You need to be seen as a professional and be able to handle tough situations. Don't forget:

- Your key messages are your safe place — use them as your armor.
- Be professional. Don't try to take on the reporter in an aggressive verbal confrontation. In the end, reporters can edit the interview any way they want.
- Be engaging, interactive, cordial and polite.
- Breathe!

Avoid these responses during an interview:

- "No comment." If you don't know an answer to a question, briefly explain to the reporter that you don't have the answer but will get back to them as quickly as possible with the information they are looking for. Or, if there's a legal or investigative reason you can't answer a question, explain it to the reporter.

- Hypotheticals. Never answer a conjectural question. Stick to the facts and stay away from "what if" questions.
- Don't repeat negatives. Avoid repeating inflammatory words in a reporter's question. For example, "How often do you hire teachers with a criminal background?" You don't want to repeat the phrase "teachers with a criminal background." Listen closely to the question and deliver a thoughtful answer.

Bridging and Flagging

There may come a time when you feel that you've lost control of the interview or need to refocus the conversation. Here are some **bridging and flagging** tips to help you get back on track and guide you to your safe place — your key messages. *Bridging* is the act of taking the reporter's off-topic question and returning to your objectives for the interview. *Flagging* is the process of emphasizing your talking points so they aren't overshadowed by misinformation or unrelated angles in the story.

Let's consider that you're in an interview in which the reporter is asking questions that may have little or nothing to do with the topic at hand, and you need to get back to your key messages. The first thing to do is *acknowledge* the question and then use one of the phrases below to *bridge* back to your messages:

- "That may be the case, but ... "
- "That's a good point, but the main consideration is ... "
- "We all agree with that, but what's at issue is ... "
- "That's not my area of expertise, but I can tell you ... "
- "As I said ... "
- "While _____ is certainly important, don't forget that ... "

Now that you are back on track and refocused, you need to use a flagging phrase that highlights your key message. Here are a few sample phrases:

- "The important point here is ... "
- "The best part about ... "
- "But the real story here is ... "
- "There are three reasons why ... "
- "Let me put it in perspective ... "
- "That speaks to a bigger point ... "

Training Tips for Engaging With Difficult Reporters

Bridging and flagging is a skill that must be practiced. During your next media training, practice use bridging and flagging techniques in a mock news interview. Have the exercise reporter approach the interviewee in an aggressive

Insights From a Media Relations Pro

Katie Wilkes has experience working with reporters all over the world, but she still relies on her training to keep her cool during intense media interviews. She shares this personal reflection of how years of media training and practice with the American Red Cross prepared her for a stressful midnight interview following a major cyclone in Mozambique.

Calm in the Eye of the Storm

In our cramped apartment, my fellow aid workers and I guessed how long the generator would hold out. It wasn't uncommon to lose power twice in a day. A sense of anticipation hung in the muggy air as I compulsively checked my messages, my polo shirt puckering from the heat.

It was my fourth week deployed to Mozambique in the spring of 2019. Cyclone Idai had pummeled Africa's southeastern coast, decimating 90% of the city of Beira, home to more than half a million people. The International Federation of Red Cross and Red Crescent Societies (IFRC) had tapped me to capture stories of survivors and raise awareness of humanitarian needs on the ground while supporting the Mozambique Red Cross.

Now, a second powerful storm, Cyclone Kenneth, battered the same coast gaining media's attention from around the world. My evening had become a balancing act providing interviews to National Public Radio, ABC News and the Associated Press. A BBC News producer sought a live broadcast interview that same night.

Years of media training had taught me to always ask for interview topics ahead of time. *Just a general update from the ground*, the producer said.

But two hours later, nearing midnight, no interview time was locked in. At the wooden kitchen table, I rehearsed my answers to the empty room before me, tapping my pen-in-hand on my right, my talking points taped to a chair on my left.

Bzzz went my phone. *Can you go live in 20?*

I flicked on the overhead lights and positioned myself in front of my phone for the Skype interview as my housemates scurried to other rooms. I'd be able to hear the producer and newscaster, but wouldn't be able to see myself. I set up a backup battery-powered light and switched to my hotspot should the power and Wi-Fi crash once again.

Through the thunderous blood pumping in my ears, I made out the newscaster's speedy questions. None of them were straightforward to answer. Panic flared inside me, then quickly subsided. Maintaining a neutral expression was difficult, yet my training held strong: *remember, you are the expert here.*

I chose to let go of what I couldn't control and bring into focus what I could: bridging to my talking points of how we were helping on the ground, how people in the path of the storm could stay safe and how others could help, too. I chose to trust myself, staring into the phone's beady pinhole camera, grounding myself with steady breaths.

What could have been another disaster turned into a timely and important story to share. Curveballs may be thrown our way, but we always have a choice to practice and become prepared. We can use our knowledge as an anchor to ground us no matter what chaos continues to swirl.

tone and ask questions that are off-topic, accusatory or attempts at soliciting opinions about another organization. The interviewee should use the bridging and flagging phrases to find their way to return to their key messages and emphasize their SOCO. These techniques are a professional and respectful way to engage with an aggressive reporter while staying on message. If you have a successful bridge and flag, the reporter will rarely bring up their off-topic questions again.

Your Phone Rings, and ... Go!

Consider this scenario: You, the media relations manager, are working on your latest project to highlight your organization's newest initiative. The phone rings. A reporter is requesting an interview with someone in your organization. The usual tendency is to start talking and answering questions, but *you do so at your own peril.*

Give yourself a chance at a successful interview. Do not immediately start answering interview questions. You need to do some quick situational analysis and determine the reason the reporter is asking questions. Is it in response to a news release you've distributed? Is it for background on a topic that is unrelated to your organization? Is the reporter looking for an SME regarding an issue in the community? Is there a crisis happening, and the reporter wants to know what your organization is doing to resolve the issue?

Listening to what the reporter is saying is important when discerning the reason for the interview. Don't listen to react; listen to *understand*. Ask yourself what is the reporter looking for and, just as important, what are they implying.

In Chapter 12, we provide a detailed checklist of what to do when a reporter calls. Here's a summary of the information you and your team must collect before you start answering questions:

- Name of the reporter.
- News outlet/agency.
- Contact information.
- The focus of the interview.
- Determine the format and location for the interview:
    - □ Television (live, recorded, in studio, on location)
    - □ Radio (live, recorded, over phone, in studio)
    - □ Print (over phone, in person, over email, on digital platforms)
    - □ Online (prerecorded for podcasts or blogs, livestreaming, written posts)

Out of respect and as a display of professionalism, ask for the reporter's deadline. You've already explained that you are unable to immediately conduct the interview, so ask what their deadline is and schedule the interview. When scheduling the interview, take into consideration how much time you need to gather the appropriate information to answer questions, identify the appropriate spokesperson and do any needed preparation such as setting up an interview location at your worksite or transporting team members to another location. Keep in mind that you still need to meet the reporter's deadline.

Note: Once you've agreed on a time for the interview, do not be late or forget to call the reporter. Your competence and trust are being scrutinized by the reporter and their news agency.

Right before you start the interview, ask the reporter when they anticipate the news item will be broadcast, published or posted. Next, be confident in the accuracy and viability of the information (i.e., key messages and talking points) you're about to share with the reporter. And be sure you brief your supervisor and leadership team before the interview and follow up with them after the interview.

ACTION STEPS

Responding to a media inquiry is not a simple task. You must carefully consider the format of the news outlet when preparing to participate in each interview. Each client or organization is going to have its own internal procedures for working with the media.

Complete the Action Steps for this chapter. Working alone or with your team members, consider how you would respond to media requests for interviews and how you would manage the many different questions they toss your way.

CHAPTER NINE ACTION STEPS: PREPARING FOR THE MEDIA INTERVIEW

Part A

Respond to the following questions to help you and your team develop your training program for managing interviews in all media formats. Refer to the chapter for tips and suggestions for addressing each situation.

1. For you and your team, what is the most important aspect of preparing for a media interview, and why? _____

2. How would you describe a SOCO for your client or organization and explain why it's so important? _____

3. What do you believe is the key to successfully delivering your message during an interview? _____

4. How would you respond to a reporter asking you a question about another organization? _____

5. How would respond to a reporter asking a hypothetical question? _____

6. What are the two most important things you need to prepare before doing a remote or online interview? _____

7. What is the one thing you do once you've delivered your key messages during an interview? _____

Part B

Develop a mini scenario based upon a current issue or event at your organization and help your team and SMEs practice answering the same questions in different media formats. Evaluate the participants based upon the particular needs of each media format (e.g., are they using shorter statements for broadcasts, more details for print, repeating the organization name for radio, and so on). Refer to Figure 9.2 for suggestions on how to practice for each format.

NOTES

[1] Erminia Fiorino, "Visual Perception, and Its Effects on Media Consumption," January 16, 2020. SMPTE. Available at https://www.smpte.org/blog/visual-perception-and-its-effect-media-consumption

Training for
News Conferences

AGENDA

1. Identify the purpose of a news conference.
2. Be deliberate in your training sessions.
3. Include all team members in planning and logistics.
4. Be strategic when inviting the media to attend.
5. Complete the Action Steps at the end of the chapter.

KEY TERMS

News Values
Media Credentials
Media Kits
Hybrid News Conference

To Have a News Conference or Not Is the Question

News conferences are orchestrated chaos: You invited members of the media to attend a meeting in which you have carefully constructed your purpose and delivered your messaging. Then you allow them to ask questions. Suddenly your control is gone, media from all types of organizations are asking questions to suit their own story development, and those who want to inquire about off-topic matters take this public opportunity to ask away.

The primary benefit of a news conference is that you can tell your story in a somewhat constructed way to all media *simultaneously*. This is important when an issue is particularly timely, such as during an emergency or when you need to make an announcement that could affect sales, stock prices or relationships with business partners. It also saves you the time you would spend doing multiple interviews, at least for the moment.

At its core, a news conference allows invited journalists to go to a designated location to listen and ask questions regarding your organization's announcement. A media relations professional uses a news conference to focus journalists' attention on very specific topics. Here are just some of the reasons you would schedule and conduct a news conference:

- To unveil a new product, service or event.
- To introduce a new CEO.
- To unveil a new business facility.
- To announce quarterly earnings.
- To respond to a controversy facing your organization.
- To give updates on a disaster or public emergency.
- To reveal a new scientific breakthrough.
- To announce an appearance by a celebrity or top government official.
- To announce a new head coach or players for a sports team.

The news conference is an important tool for a media relations professional, but only if it's useful to the organization's mission and communication plan. Some media relations professionals may go through their entire careers without conducting a single news conference. Other communicators may host one on special occasions, and still others may conduct news conferences with such regularity that it's a normal business occurrence (e.g., the White House or a professional sports team).

Do We Need to Train for News Conferences?

Before you decide if news conferences should be part of your media relations training program, you need to determine: (1) what would be the purpose? and (2) how often would you need to host one? If you answer the following questions and don't see a lot of use for news conferences in your media relations plan, then perhaps you don't need to invest the time and resources in training for one.

- **Is the information newsworthy?** Whether for a special occasion or an everyday event, the foundation for all successful news conferences is ensuring the information is *newsworthy*. Your organization's announcement must be of such significance as to entice journalists to take time out of their busy schedules, travel to a specific location at a specific time, participate in the news conference and then choose to report on it. Your announcement should address or include at least one of the following **news values**: *impact, proximity, prominence, timeliness, unique/bizarre, conflict, currency*

PETER MACIAS
AMERICAN RED CROSS

AFTERMATH OF
MICHAEL

WVTM
13

HURRICANE
HELP

WVTM13.COM
DONATE ONLINE

American
Red Cross

Peter Macías (right) represented the American Red Cross in a joint news conference with a FEMA sign language interpreter to update reporters on the Hurricane Michael response efforts in October 2018. Collaboration with all partners involved in disaster response efforts is essential for ensuring accurate and timely information is shared during media opportunities such as this one. **PHOTO CREDIT: J. SUZANNE HORSLEY.**

and human interest. If you can't articulate how your news would impact your external publics, then it is not newsworthy.

- **Is the timing right?** Are you too early in the development of this fascinating concept that you won't have all the answers to reporters' questions? Is it so far away from launch time that the public would forget by then? Conversely, have you already announced the news through social media, advertisements or other communication methods, leaving no advantage to a media event?

- **Will the media be available?** Don't plan a big announcement during the prime broadcast news hours in the afternoon and evening. Don't expect media to show up on a Friday afternoon or weekend unless there is a truly compelling reason for the timing. Exceptions to these rules may include law enforcement announcements that could protect public safety or updates about events that are so traumatic or life changing that you must share it at once. Don't try to compete with larger news stories in your local or national markets. The media have limited resources and will choose the more important story.

Preparing for In-Person News Conferences

Once you determine that news conferences will be an important part of your media relations plan, your next step should be to include all your team members in the planning and preparation. It is essential to conduct training and rehearsal that includes all planning essentials so there are no surprises when you host media events. The checklist for "News Conference Planning" will help you prepare a customized plan for your media events and identify all team members who should be included in the training.

Checklist: News Conference Planning

Review the questions posed in the following list to determine what you would need to include in your own plan:

✓ **Timeline:** How much advanced notice do you have? Does your organization typically have breaking news events, or do you have months to plan an announcement? How often do you foresee needing to schedule a news conference? Based upon the type of announcement you will deliver, what is the best day and time to schedule it?

✓ **Message and Delivery:** Who will develop the talking points for your news conference? Who will be the designated spokesperson? Do you anticipate bringing in partnering organizations to participate in your news conference?

✓ **Message Training for the Spokesperson or SME:** Who from your team will train and rehearse with the spokespersons and SMEs who participate in the news conference?

✓ **Collateral Materials:** Who are the individuals assigned to create **media kits** that contain speaker information, biographies, news releases, fact sheets and other materials that will be shared with reporters at the news conference?

✓ **Media Invitations and Credentialing:** Who is the team member charged with selecting and inviting journalists to your news conference? If your news conference requires tight control of attendees due to security, you should assign a team member to manage the credentialing of all members of the news media. Depending upon the level of security, this may include anything from conducting background checks on reporters to requesting letters from employers that verify an individual is reporting for their news organization.

✓ **Logistics:** Who from your team is detail-oriented and understands event planning well enough to manage news conference logistics? This includes a variety of details from selecting the location, installing branding visuals and staging speakers, to placing directional signs, setting up an audio mult box and making sure there are enough power outlets for the media. Does the location provide an anteroom for the speakers and team members to gather before the event? Does the podium have a microphone, sound system and branding that will be visible in video and still shots? If your news conference will be so large that it will be difficult for reporters to see the stage, is a riser available to put at the back of the room for videographers and photographers?

✓ **News Conference Check-in Table:** Which team members will be assigned to greet the media, check **media credentials** if necessary and log attendees' names and contact information? Do they have the necessary knowledge of

(continued)

the video and sound equipment on scene to help reporters set up mics or pooled video? Who from the team will check in all speakers, provide key messages and updated talking points and support the presenters?

✓ **Welcome and Introductions:** Which member of your team will start the news conference with a greeting, a statement of purpose, and introductions of speakers? Who will moderate the question-and-answer session that follows? Who will keep time to ensure that no one speaks too long and that the event ends on schedule? And who is keeping track of reporters' questions that require follow-up?

Virtual and Hybrid News Conferences

As noted previously, video conferencing platforms that are relatively inexpensive and easy to use have made it less urgent for the media and the organization members to be in the same room for a news conference. This also gives you an advantage when you want coverage from national or international media. If you're dealing with a small media budget, a small staff or a global media environment, it is likely you would plan a news conference that either eliminates the need for everyone to be present in the same physical location, meaning the conference is completely virtual, or that allows participants to attend in person or virtually **(hybrid news conference).**

Virtual and hybrid news conferences have particular challenges and require a set of logistical skills that are different from in-person news conferences. In addition to the news conference planning checklist above, you also need to consider the following in your training plan:

- **Technical Expertise:** Who will be assigned to manage all technical aspects of this virtual event? Who will provide the computers, video conferencing programs, cameras and audio equipment for your speakers? Do you need someone to livestream this event on your social media platform or website?

- **Security:** How will you allow media representatives to register and enter the virtual news conference? How will you ensure "Zoom bombers" (individuals who attempt to disrupt an online event) will be blocked? Will your server be protected from hackers?

- **Media Kits:** Who is responsible for ensuring all materials provided for the media are distributed electronically or available for download? Will the materials be password protected or publicly accessible?

As you determine your logistical needs for future news conferences, add these considerations to your media relations training plan to ensure your team is always ready when it's time to make important news announcements.

Insights From a Media Relations Pro

As we mentioned earlier in this chapter, some media relations pros never have a need for news conferences, while others may plan them on a regular basis. Renee Felton, the head of communications for USA Basketball, routinely holds news conferences. She offers her advice for this important media relations activity, especially in light of the global coronavirus epidemic.

Planning News Conferences During Uncertain Times

Having spent my career in sports and nonprofit communication, I know the value of a news conference to place important news in front of a large and diverse group of media. News conferences require coordination and attention to detail, but they are worth it for the amount of media attention an event can garner. It's important to remember that not every announcement merits a news conference — sometimes all you need is a news release, a tweet or a few calls to your friendly local media.

In sports, we use news conferences, or variations of them, in a variety of ways. In the COVID-19 era (more on that later), we have had to rethink our media operations nearly 100%, but news conferences and media availabilities haven't gone anywhere.

For my organization, the most valuable use of a news conference is to introduce new personnel — leadership, coaching staff, free agent signees and trade acquisitions. Media yearn to get face time with these folks, and a news conference is a great way to get someone in front of a big group. After the main event, take time to introduce your new faces to the media, and consider who should get some one-on-one time for interviews afterward. It can make for a long day, but it's your job to ensure your new coworkers understand the value of spending a few hours with the media and regularly check in with them in the future. In some cases, this media expectation will be written into their contracts.

When planning a news conference, I consider a few things:

1. **Location:** You need a place that can accommodate a large group and has the proper tech support for TV and radio affiliates.

2. **Schedule:** Don't schedule an important announcement when it could be overshadowed by another event or media obligation. For me, that's making sure that we aren't trying to schedule a media event at the same time we know another sports team in town holds standing media availability, has a game or has a lot of media traveling with them on the road. You also want to schedule to complement local live news broadcasts. I've always found that mid-morning is a good time.

3. **Coordination:** Your team might be responsible for the nuts-and-bolts of the news conference, but interdepartmental coordination is important (social media, event planning, marketing, etc.).

4. **Stage Presence:** Who needs a voice in the announcement or introduction? You don't want to overload the stage with guests, but the organization needs to be properly represented. Don't forget to include a moderator (which could be you).

5. **Run of Show:** I always like to give each participant the opportunity to make an opening statement before starting the Q&A. Don't forget to have someone available to pass microphones among the media so everyone in the room can hear questions.

6. **Talking Points:** If you don't take another thing away from this entire spiel, please remember that you must set up your news conference participants to succeed. It's your job to make sure everyone is comfortable, prepared and has considered any sticky subjects that could arise.

(continued)

> **A Word on COVID-19:** One positive (dare I say) to adjusting media operations in COVID-19 times is that we have the ability to be virtually present, news conferences included. Consider if your event would benefit from a virtual component (Zoom, Microsoft Teams, or livestreaming) in which people who can't be in the room can still participate, ask questions and hear directly from the horse's mouth. Geography, positive COVID-19 tests, schedule conflicts and participant safety are just a few of the factors that can help you make that decision. In fact, if the situation is really crazy, a 100% virtual news conference is always possible.

ACTION STEPS

As you learn more about preparing for a news conference, you can add this information to your media relations training program. The criteria your media relations team establishes for deciding whether to host a news conference should be the first step, followed by planning and logistical considerations for this highly visible media activity. The media relations team members should be part of every step of this planning to ensure everyone contributes their expertise and understands their role for implementation.

Complete the Action Steps for this chapter, which help you establish your criteria for hosting a news conference, develop the plan for implementing a news conference and create the training component for your team.

CHAPTER TEN ACTION STEPS:
ESTABLISH YOUR ORGANIZATION'S POLICIES AND PROCEDURES
FOR NEWS CONFERENCES

Part A

On your own or with your media relations team members, review the mission, vision, values and strategic plan of your organization or client. Then consider the following questions that will help you develop a news conference policy:

1. When was the last time your organization or client held a news conference? What were the results, such as the number of journalists in attendance, the assessment of resulting media coverage, or other factors you can measure? _____

2. Does your organization often have news announcements that merit the investment of time and resources in a news conference? If so, give some examples. _____

3. Are there opportunities in the future that would benefit from simultaneous announcements in front of all your key media? _____

4. After assessing your organization's past use of and future need for news conferences, draft a policy for determining if and when a news conference will be used for future newsworthy announcements: _____

Part B

1. If news conferences would benefit your organization's strategic goals, develop a plan that includes everything from decision-making indicators to event logistics.

   a. What are the associated news values? _____

   b. Will you conduct an in-person, virtual or hybrid news conference? _____

   c. Will you livestream this event? _____

   d. What are the top three talking points? _____

   e. Who are the moderator, spokesperson(s) and SME(s)? _____

   f. Are there any partner organizations you should invite to join? _____

   g. Do you have an updated media roster for inviting members of the media? _____

   h. What are the logistical challenges (venue size, electronic equipment, security, tech for hybrid presentation)? _____

   i. What is the best day and time to host your news conference? Have you consulted with the executive team to ensure they are available? Have you checked for competing events that would prevent media from attending? _____

   Note: Get creative! Add more questions that support your organization's unique operating environment.

2. Create a chart of news conference roles and responsibilities. Then assign a role/responsibility to each media relations team member, spokesperson, SME, leader, tech specialist and anyone else from your organization who must be included for a successful event.

   Example (feel free to modify to fit your organization's needs):

Role/Responsibility	Team Member #1	Team Member #2
Book the venue	Abernathy	
Check leadership calendars	Dover	
Write talking points	Poole	Johnson
Train spokespersons/SMEs	Jackson	Wade
Invite media	Ramirez	
Credential media	Sanders	
Moderate	Ahmad	
Etc.		

Creating Simulations and Scenarios

KEY CONCEPTS

Simulations
Scenario Development
Scenario Inject
Evaluation

Why Use Simulations in Media Training?

We have mentioned the importance of practice and rehearsal throughout this handbook, but this chapter goes deeper into making those rehearsals as realistic as possible. You, as the media relations lead, will find yourself responsible for ensuring the quality capabilities of your spokespersons and subject matter experts. The only way to test your team members' abilities to deliver effective messaging, maintain a professional demeanor and successfully represent your organization is to create and schedule a media training. Not only will the media training help hone their interview skills, it will also test their critical thinking skills and allow them to do so in a safe learning environment. The key to a successful media training exercise is all in the planning and creativity of the event.

As we've explained in earlier chapters, media training is a gathering of a spokesperson team to review the latest in organizational messaging, practice interview skills during simulated media interviews, clarify each team member's roles and responsibilities and become familiar with the latest in interview techniques. The value of going beyond a basic tabletop exercise in which each participant simply discusses what they would do in certain situations is that **simulations** create a real-world experience in which participants will feel emotions as they navigate the exercise. Participants in our training exercises have reported feeling nervous, overwhelmed, joyous, scared, excited, confused — a full range of emotions that can bolster the learning in that moment.

As trainers, we want our participants to *feel* what it's like to be under pressure, to dig into their memories for key facts and to construct thoughtful responses while facing a reporter with a microphone and camera. Media training exercises allow spokespersons the chance to practice how to stay on message, prepare for a variety of possible interview formats, manage and think through unexpected questions and use interview locations to their advantage. They also force the participant to do all these things in a fast-paced environment instead of at their leisure.

The number of spokespersons being trained can vary from hundreds to a single person. The only limitations are budget, logistics and creativity. Media training will pinpoint the strengths and weaknesses of each spokesperson, cultivate their skills, solidify your spokesperson roster and help you develop a plan of action for calling upon your spokespersons. Ultimately, the exercises will help the trainees identify the skills they should focus on to become proficient spokespersons.

Before you jump into **scenario development**, establish some ground rules. Everyone involved should understand the expectations of this activity:

- All participants are expected to "play along" with the scenario and remain in their roles throughout the exercises. From our experience as trainers, the participants who refuse to take the exercises seriously are also the ones who are the least successful spokespersons.

- Participants are expected to train within the established parameters of the scenario and agree to be part of the conversation during the review process.

- Facilitators are expected to manage the flow of the exercise and encourage the trainees to help each other with suggestions, solutions and peer coaching.

- Evaluators are expected to identify trainees' strengths and areas for improvement while providing constructive, positive feedback.

Insights From a Media Relations Pro	*It takes countless details and unbounded creativity to make a training exercise realistic and beneficial for all participants. Tammie Pech, an award-winning public relations practitioner with experience training spokespersons for national and international disaster response, shares her process of developing high-level training experiences.*

Planning Realistic Exercises That Challenge Your Team

When planning the training, think through the logistics of how many are being trained; if only a few people, a single room may work. If training a large group, you may need a facility that has several rooms. You can split a large group of trainees into teams to cycle through the different types of interviews (virtual, IFB or in person). A media hub is recommended for viewing trainees and recording interviews while they are being conducted. A separate room for those waiting to be interviewed should have a live feed screen, so that those waiting can evaluate their peers and provide feedback.

Each practice interview should be conducted as if "live" with the media outlet. Trainees should be briefed prior to each round of interviews about the expectation of the interview and tips for managing the reporter. Some suggestions include:

- Words or phrases to use or avoid.
- Incident-specific talking points for accurate messaging.
- Personal appearance and branding.
- Nonverbal interview techniques (e.g., look at the camera if virtual or IFB but look at the reporter if in person.
- Strategies for blocking negative questions and bridging back to the talking points.
- Tips for staying calm during a contentious interview.
- Each interview should last approximately 2-3 minutes with post-evaluation lasting approximately 3-5 minutes.

Training materials should include:

- The written scenario.
- Specific talking points or organizational key messages.
- Evaluation cards for peers and for the training evaluators.
- Potential **scenario injects** prior to each interview (injects are plot twists that are added during the scenario to force the trainees to practice adjusting their messaging).

Evaluators will need a copy of the scenario and any additional injects, a list of suggested topics or areas that the trainers want to focus on, and something to note "best of the best" for each type of interview. Prior to training, it is important for the training coordinator to meet with all evaluators and reporters to provide an outline of outcomes you want to see from the trainees.

Overall, you want the training experience to stretch each of the participants' abilities but still be a valuable and worthwhile experience. Creating no-win scenarios for the trainees will not reinforce active learning. To help with this, you may consider offering a postinterview highlight session to review examples of strong interviews, ensure that evaluators are offering constructive suggestions for future interviews, and provide at least some positive feedback on every interview. You want the trainees to leave feeling empowered to give a good interview for your organization, not feeling fearful and defeated.

The Scenario

To put a spokesperson's skills to the test, you need to create a customized real-world scenario that will *challenge* their:

- Capability to deliver their message (reinforcing the single overriding communication objective — SOCO — while blending facts and human interest to deliver a compelling story).
- Ability to adapt to an unexpected change in a situation (such as a scenario inject or sudden accusations by the reporter).
- Ability to use their surroundings as part of the story (for example, mention that they are in a foodbank warehouse while talking about food insecurity).
- Ability to stay professional during a hostile interview (remain calm, respectful and on message while the reporter asks negative questions).
- Ability to use their talking points as their focal point (avoid taking the bait from a reporter who wants to take the story in a different direction).

The best media interview scenarios are those that reflect real-life business or work situations related to your organization. For example, if your organization provides first responder services, you may want to develop a simulation that incorporates some type of disaster: house fire, tornado, active shooter, hurricane, hazmat spill, wildfire or earthquake. Each of these disasters will serve as an opportunity to test even the most seasoned spokesperson. In this case, you may want to invite partner emergency response agencies to participate in this exercise and practice multiagency media relations.

Here is a sample scenario with updates that emerge during the exercise to make it more challenging:

> *You work for a small county government in the Midwest with a population of 105,000 residents. Most of the population, 75,000, live in the county seat where you work. The county seat happens to be the location for a large railroad hub. Trains that crisscross the country are carrying everything from grain, livestock, lumber, coal, chemicals, autos and auto parts, materials to build homes, and people. A railroad spur leading to the hub runs within a mile of two elementary schools, a senior living facility and a shopping center.*
>
> *At 11:20 a.m. a train derails on the spur, and two of the cars end up on their sides spewing an unknown gas into the air. Police and the volunteer fire department are responding. The county emergency management operations center is being activated.*
>
> *A weather front is blowing through and causing a plume of gas to start drifting toward one of the elementary schools and the senior living facility. As a precaution, the county emergency manager calls for all citizens east of the derailment site to shelter in place.*

News of the derailment is getting out to the public. The news media have been contacted to ask residents and businesses in the path of the gas plume to shelter in place. Parents are in a panic because they can't get to their children at the elementary school. Relatives of the nursing home residents are in a panic because they cannot get to their loved ones.

The local, state and national news media are calling you for information. News crews are showing up at multiple sites.

This scenario, although broad in scope, has enough variables to test even the most seasoned spokesperson's skills. You could also add injects or updates to the scenario as the interviews progress, such as:

- Changes in the weather or known dangers occur as the response develops.
- Revelations that the initial group of first responders were injured.
- Spokespersons from the railroad company arrive and attempt to preempt blame.
- The Federal Railway Administration investigators arrive on scene.
- People are showing up at the local hospital with medical conditions possibly related to the release of the toxic gas.
- Traffic is becoming an issue because of road closures, preventing school buses from taking children home.
- An elderly resident has locked himself in his car because he is afraid of being exposed to the toxic gas cloud.
- The governor's office is calling your agency for status reports.

The possibilities of plot twists and additional challenges to completing the interviews are numerous. Just remember Tammie Pech's advice — make the scenario challenging, but not insurmountable for the participants.

Inviting Professional Guests to the Training

There is a certain feeling of uneasiness from not being in control during a media interview. It takes a bit of courage to stand up and represent an organization knowing that you are the "face of the company." It takes a little extra courage to keep your faculties about you and stay on message while responding to unexpected questions, especially when the questions are outside the scope of your prepared messaging.

To enhance the media training exercise, consider inviting professional journalists and veteran spokespersons from other organizations to serve as coaches and evaluators. Their experience and perspective will afford the trainees a chance to hear firsthand what a journalist expects from the interviewee. Their coaching will also help a naïve spokesperson overcome the uneasiness of being interviewed by a reporter.

You should also hire a professional videographer to record the interviews and produce high-quality clips for the review session. Have a few monitors in a separate room for participants to watch and learn from each other. Invite the videographer to share tips from their perspective behind the camera, such as:

- Should the interviewee have their own IFB earpiece?
- What is the best color or pattern of clothing to wear?
- What do they recommend about using makeup or wearing jewelry?
- What should the interviewee do if they're noticeably perspiring?
- Where should the interviewee look during the interview?
- What are some considerations regarding wearing hats, jackets or shirts with the organization's branding on them?
- When is the best time to pitch another story?

Every bit of advice provided to a spokesperson will give them a better opportunity to succeed and provide a quality interview in the future.

Chris Osborne, a former broadcast journalist and current communication manager for a public health agency, shared his expertise with students during a media training exercise at The University of Alabama in April 2022. Osborne helped students find ways to manage their body language and prioritize their talking points during mock interviews. Afterward, Osborne and other media trainers shared their critiques with the students. **PHOTO CREDIT: J. SUZANNE HORSLEY.**

Don't Rest on Your Laurels

Have you heard the phrase, "You're only as good as your last win"? Anyone can have an off day and deliver a mediocre interview. The bad interview may have resulted from one of these situations:

- You got nervous before the interview.
- You forgot to deliver an important part of your messaging.
- The reporter started asking rapid-fire questions and tossed you off your game.
- The reporter asked questions totally outside the scope of the interview.
- The reporter used long exaggerated pauses between questions; there was an uncomfortable silence, and you felt the need to fill the silence by rambling.
- The reporter asked for a comment regarding another organization.
- The reporter asked you a hypothetical question.
- At the end of the interview, the reporter made a negative comment on camera that you were not able to respond to.

There can be any number of reasons for a bad interview, but by preparing and practicing, a potential spokesperson can significantly increase the likelihood of a successful interview.

Interview Tips

Focus on your answers, not the questions:

- Reporters ask anything they like; you can answer any way you like.
- You don't have to answer a question, but you *do* have to deliver the message.
- Provide facts and examples to support your messaging.
- Good anecdotes make the story come alive.
- Be professional, engaging and polite.
- Your key messages are your safe place.

Evaluating the Interviews

Long before the training begins, the participants should understand exactly what the judging criteria are and how they will be evaluated. As the coordinator for the media training, you'll need to determine what traits and skills they need to demonstrate when representing the organization during the interview. Below is a list of possible evaluation points:

- Message delivery
  - ☐ Successfully conveys the corporate messaging by using the talking points.
  - ☐ Successfully answers the reporter's questions.

☐ Provides supporting facts, stories and examples.

☐ Provides detail and sentiment to humanize the message.

☐ Uses bridging phrases to redirect off-topic questions back to the main subject, such as:

　. . . yes that's true, but you should know . . .

　. . . what's really important is . . .

　. . . that's one way to look at it, but another way . . .

☐ Provides a call to action for the public.

- Demeanor

　☐ Is cordial, professional and engaging.

　☐ Speaks clearly and succinctly.

　☐ Acts calm and collected.

　☐ Looks at the reporter (or at the camera if no reporter).

　☐ Uses appropriate hand gestures and facial expressions.

- Physical appearance

　☐ Is dressed appropriately/professionally for the interview.

　☐ Is properly branded.

　☐ Is able to reduce the appearance of excessive perspiration.

　☐ Hair and makeup are appropriate for the circumstances.

The training is wasted if the participants don't have access to constructive feedback from the evaluators and from their peers. Each spokesperson who goes through the training should be given an evaluation right after the interviews. The feedback should be clear and specific, as it offers positive and not-so-positive examples from the interview. The evaluator should also share tips for improvement while being honest, supportive and motivational.

Evaluating the Training Session

Media trainers need to know what worked and what didn't work for the participants. Gathering feedback from the participants will allow you to tweak elements for the next media training session. Here are some sample questions that generate feedback:

- Did the training provide you an opportunity to successfully practice your skills?

- Was the scenario challenging enough for you to stretch your abilities?

- Was the evaluator knowledgeable?

- Did you receive constructive feedback from your evaluator?

- Was the training facility satisfactory?

- What would you want to learn in your next phase of training?

ACTION STEPS

Developing media training scenarios for your organization or client is a serious endeavor. You will use the organization's money, resources and personnel to conduct your training while asking the participants to give you their time away from their daily responsibilities. You want the final product to be valuable for the whole organization.

Work with your team to develop a meaningful training opportunity for your spokespersons, SMEs and leadership. Determine your goals for the training activity and be sure you can meet those goals with the resources, trainers and evaluators you bring to the session.

Complete the Action Steps for this chapter. Determine the logistics you need to create a successful training exercise and the elements you want to include. Use this chapter's Action Steps for creative brainstorming as you develop a scenario to test your colleagues' proficiencies at participating in challenging interviews.

CHAPTER ELEVEN ACTION STEPS: CREATING THE TRAINING EXPERIENCE

Part A

Determine the personnel, resources and logistics necessary to implement your media interview simulations:

1. Who in your organization needs to be part of your media training and why? The individuals would include those who fill all roles necessary to implement your training. _____
2. What logistical steps would you take to set up a media training? Be specific as you think through the procedures necessary to plan a training activity for your organization, including scheduling, extending internal invitations, hiring outside consultants, obtaining budget approvals, determining the location, and staffing. _____
3. Referring back to Chapter 9, what types of interview formats would be most valuable for this training? _____
4. What training materials (e.g., key messages, talking points, scenario injects, maps, evaluation forms, situation reports, media rosters, media alerts and so on) need to be developed and provided for the participants (e.g., reporters, evaluators and trainees)? _____
5. Who would you invite to take the training, and why? _____
6. Which communication professionals would you invite to serve as the reporters, camera operators, evaluators or coaches? _____

Part B

Create a scenario for your client or organization that you will use for the training exercise. Remember to follow the tips in this chapter to make the scenario realistic and beneficial for your organization. Include scenario injects that will make your trainees think on their feet. The scenario should be detailed enough that the reporters will have ample questions to ask each participant, and it should be challenging enough for your trainees to work hard to recall details and talking points while working to stay on message.

Part C

Conduct a pilot test with a small group from your team or organization. Based on the scenario you created, have your participants test their messaging and delivery. Have them practice delivering the key messages and talking points that are based on your SOCO for a variety of interview formats. Assess the information you collected in Part A to determine if anything was missing or unnecessary. Solicit feedback from your pilot participants and finalize the simulation details and materials. Once you are comfortable with your logistics and format, you are ready for your training exercises.

Checklists and Resources

Your Media Relations Training Toolbox

The training experiences that you create for your organization will also help *you* become more prepared. The more time you spend anticipating the needs of your media relations team, the more prepared you personally will be with the policies, procedures, messaging and resources that you have learned about in this handbook.

There are a variety of resources that you want your media relations team to always have easy access to in your **media relations training toolbox**. You may want to consider having an online resource (such as an internal webpage, file storage account or Google docs, for example) that are password protected but readily available to your team.

Here's a list of resources to get you started:

- Internal documents
  - ☐ These include your media relations philosophy, strategic communication plans, media relations training documents, policies and procedures for conducting media relations work in your organization, media kit contents, and prewritten key messages and talking points.
  - ☐ Contact information for all media relations team members, key executives, spokespeople and SMEs.
  - ☐ Data, reports and executive summaries from your communication and media coverage audits.
  - ☐ Media inquiry databases or spreadsheets, easily accessible for logging in new calls or for researching reporters.
  - ☐ Up-to-date media lists and documents of vetted spokespeople and trained SMEs to ensure your team is calling upon the right people for the right interview.
  - ☐ Plans for providing accommodations for people of all abilities and for hiring language translators.
  - ☐ The end-of-chapter Action Steps in this book are also great information resources as your team continues to develop your media relations training program.
- Associated Press Stylebook
  - ☐ If you want to work in media relations, you need to speak the journalists' language. Provide hard copies or online subscriptions[1] to the most recent version of the AP Stylebook for all members of your team. Include written exercises to test your team members' knowledge of AP style in your training activities.
- Codes of Ethics
  - ☐ Professional communication and news media membership associations are guided by written codes of ethics that all members must adhere to. Even if you are not a member yourself, you cannot operate in this realm without full knowledge of the expected codes of conduct. Review the codes of ethics for communication associations as well as industry-specific ones for your line of work.
    - ▪ Public Relations Society of America (www.prsa.org).
    - ▪ The National Association of Government Communicators (https://nagc.com/).
    - ▪ The Society of Professional Journalists (www.spj.org)
- Training and Development Resources
  - ☐ The professional membership associations listed above are also a great source of materials for developing new skills, reading case studies and learning the latest in technological developments for your field. Some resources are free, while others require a membership or a fee.

☐ Membership organizations for your specific industry are also a vital resource of current information, training opportunities and legal or regulatory updates. Always be a student of your industry to ensure you can represent your line of work in all media interview opportunities.

- Mentorship Opportunities
  ☐ Providing mentorship for your media relations team members gives them the opportunity to practice for upcoming interviews, debrief after difficult interviews or share the ups and downs of media relations work. Create a formal mechanism for members of your team to be a mentor or mentee; the mentors can also come from partner organizations, different field offices or your organization's pool of retirees.

Checklists for Your Media Relations Training Toolbox

We hope that you have found some valuable information in this handbook to help you develop a robust media training program for your client or organization. In the Action Steps at the end of the chapter are some of the most important tips that we've compiled into convenient starter checklists. These checklists should be included in all your media training activities and be available on-demand for the media relations team.

Checklist topics include:

- References to your organization's mission, vision, values and objectives to ensure all your media relations activities are complementing these strategies.
- Media relations team rosters and roles with contact information.
- Prepared key messages and talking points.
- Up-to-date media lists.
- List of verified spokespersons, subject matter experts and third-party verifiers with contact details.
- Inventory of materials, equipment and human resources needed for media relations training simulations.
- Policies and procedures that you developed for crisis response.
- Database for tracking media inquiries.
- Procedures for triaging and assigning media calls.
- Crisis communication collateral materials.
- Plans for a crisis command center.
- Plans for your team's participation in a joint information center.
- Key messages and talking points documents for specific situations.
- Checklists for interviews in different media formats.

- Checklists for news conference logistics.
- Inventory of training materials, including evaluation forms and interview tips.

It may seem like a lot of work to prepare these checklists for your training program, but the greatest benefit is that these materials will be current and readily available when your team members are ready to do their interviews. They will train with the exact same materials that they will use when the real reporters call.

Just remember: Strong key messages, talking points and pages of checklists do not automatically result in successful media interviews. The *human component* is a must, and without the ability to tell your story with compassion and empathy, no one will believe you, much less remember you. Consider this advice from media relations pro Katie Wilkes in our final case study.

Insights From a Media Relations Pro

When checking off lists to be prepared for your media exercises, and eventually the real deal, don't forget that the way you represent the human experience will be the one thing that your audiences will remember beyond all facts and figures. Katie Wilkes shares this personal reflection of how she works to keep compassion and empathy at the forefront of her media interviews.

At the Heart of the Media Matter

"I've got this," I thought. "Just a routine live shot, and I know the facts like the back of my hand."

It was my final interview on the ground after six months of helping people recover from the strongest storm on record to ever strike the Bahamas. Scars left by Hurricane Dorian remained raw, yet the memory had dissipated in much of the world's mind.

I have spent more than a decade seeking stories of resilience with the world's largest humanitarian network. Embedded beneath my skin are imprints of hundreds of eyewitness accounts, including a mother's eyes grieving her lost sons, and children sifting through debris for their books. These unspeakable truths transcend languages and borders and are often reduced to fractions within 30-second broadcast clips.

To give an interview is to speak in the name of survivors and victims. It's a duty and an honor I take to heart. Each of these stories has become my "why" when I speak to the media. Now I needed to remind the public that disasters don't go away after the news crews do.

Between roaring generators and echoes of convening aid workers, I perched my camera's tripod in a relatively quiet parking lot corner, feet planted in my power stance.

"And three, two ... " the producer chirped through my earbuds, signaling we were live. B-roll footage I had shot depicting piled debris rippled across my small screen. Even if I forgot the stats, I would speak to what I knew, images fresh in my mind. It would be smooth sailing.

Until it wasn't. Piercing static erupted in my ears as the anchor introduced me. The feedback was so blaring I couldn't hear myself talk. I made out every fifth word. *Something about needs. Another about progress. Did he say biggest hurdle or biggest turtle?*

Although I couldn't hear the reporter's questions clearly, I still could decipher stories speaking from within me. I spoke of the father we spent months searching for to deliver critical aid, who was now empowered to begin working again to support his family. His voice was one of many deserving to be amplified.

(continued)

Just then, something brushed my ankle. A stray cat leapt, figure-eighting through my legs. A teammate passed in front of my camera, waved and motioned a thumbs-up. The roar of a jet engine crescendoed above me. A four-minute interview felt like 30, one of those "couldn't tell you what I just said" moments.

My team would later tell me, *"Katie, we cheered watching your interview! You crushed it!"*

We are our own worst critics, minimizing small victories and maximizing flubs. No matter how much distraction tries to pierce our message, authenticity will always speak louder than memorized statistics. "Just the facts, ma'am," are just words floating without color.

A story worth sharing is a story spoken from the heart — what does it make us feel? Because that's when we'll know, *we've got this.*

ACTION STEPS

If you have completed all the chapters and Action Steps in this handbook, you should have the beginnings of a well-planned media relations training program that you can develop further and implement for your organization.

Complete the Action Steps for this chapter. Using the starter templates provided, create your own checklists that will be used by the media relations training organizers, participants, spokespersons and SMEs. Add these checklists to your media relations training toolbox so that your team will be ready to respond when the media call.

CHAPTER TWELVE ACTION STEPS:
CHECKLISTS FOR SUCCESSFUL MEDIA TRAINING

We have compiled some of the most important tips presented throughout this handbook into convenient checklists. These checklists are intended to be starting points for you and your team members to customize and develop to suit the mission, vision, values and objectives of your organization. Feel free to add, subtract, rearrange or reconstruct them to be as useful as possible for your training objectives.

We recommend that you produce your own materials and make them accessible to all members of your team. Before each training activity, take a fresh look at the media relations training program you developed and see what you might need to update or expand upon.

1. **Connecting Your Media Relations Work to Organizational Strategy.** For each media opportunity, ensure it is supporting your client's or organization's strategic priorities by connecting the topics, medium (news outlet) and story angles back to your mission, vision, values and objectives. Check off where your strategic priorities align with the media opportunity.

	Mission	Vision	Values	Objectives
Topic				
Reporter's story focus				
Medium				
News outlet's target audience				
Other considerations				

2. **Media Relations Team Roster and Roles.** Maintain updated rosters to ensure you can reach the right team members for the appropriate role at any time. Fill in the specific needs for each role.

	MR logistics and tech support	Spokesperson	SME (include areas of expertise)	External partners or third-party verifiers
Team member A Contact info				
Team member B Contact info				
Team member C Contact info				

3. **Inventory of Prepared Key Messages (KM) and Talking Points (TP) for a Variety of Topics.** Keep a list of all available documents to make it easy for team members to search for the required information before developing new material. Insert document names (or hyperlinks to electronic documents) as an easy locator tool for the correct document — this table shows examples of how to list the resources. Add more rows and columns to match the documents you have available.

	Organization backgrounder	Organization history	New product line details	New leadership bios	FAQs
KM	Backgrounder.doc	History.doc			For the organization
TP			Product2023.doc	PresidentBio.doc	For new initiatives or crisis events

4. **Media Lists.** Your media lists should have complete information so that you can create targeted lists for specific news announcements. Add more columns to customize your searches for the best media for each issue.

Reporter	News Outlet	Phone	Email	Preferred contact method	Website	Primary news beat	Last contact

5. **Materials and Resources for Training Checklists.** The Action Steps in Chapter 6 asked you to generate lists of the material and human resources you would need for your desired level of training simulations (entry, professional or moderate levels). Take your current inventory from Part A of those Action Steps, add the resources you are able to add from Part B and create a checklist of all the items and people you need for a successful media training experience.

6. **Policies and Procedures.** For each policy that you have (or need to create) that guides your media relations program, compile an inventory that includes the approval dates for each document.

   - Procedures for tracking media inquiries.
   - Policy for triaging and responding to media calls.
   - Procedures for internal crisis command center.
   - Procedures for participating in a joint information center

7. **Inventory of Support Documents.** Create a checklist that contains all available support documents, date of latest update and list of documents still needed to be assigned for development.

   - Crisis communication collateral materials.
   - Key messages (evergreen documents such as organization history, bios of leaders and overviews of products and services).
   - Talking points (documents that have facts, figures and details for specific events that are nonroutine or rapidly evolving, including new product launches, changes in leadership, and crisis events).

8. **Checklist for Giving Interviews in Different Media Formats.** In Chapter 9 we provided charts to describe how to work with media in print, broadcast and online formats. The way you work with reporters in each format will change the way you prepare and deliver your information. Use the charts to create checklists to help your spokespeople prepare for the next interview opportunity.

9. **Checklist for News Conference Logistics.**

News Conference Items	Team member in charge	Details
Identified news values		
In-person, virtual or hybrid		
Option for livestreaming		
Top three talking points		
Moderator		
Spokesperson(s)		
SME(s)		
Partner organizations		
Media invitations		
Venue		
Technology needs		
Site security		
Credentialing of media		
Confirmed date and time		
Confirmed schedule with leadership		
Any events competing for media attention		
Additional specifics for your event		
An accessibility coordinator for Deaf interpreters, language translators, and mobility accommodations.		

10. **Inventory of Training Materials.** As you generate materials for your media training simulations in Chapter 11, create an inventory of all items, including the file locations and last update. Materials — at minimum — will include the scenario, talking points, scenario injects, evaluation forms for trainers and peer evaluation forms.

NOTE

[1]   Available at https://www.apstylebook.com/

Index